THE BOOK OF LIFE

THE BOOK OF LIFE

Pura Regalado

Kravitz & Sons

Kravitz and Sons LLC
1301 Farmville Blvd, Suite 104
Greenville, NC 27834

Published by Kravitz and Sons LLC.
ISBN: 979-8-89639-096-1 (sc)

Library of Congress Control Number: 2025903460

CONTENTS

CHAPTER 1

THE COLLECTIVE UNCONSCIOUS

Have you ever heard of the phenomenon of the collective unconscious? Have you ever heard of the archetype that emanates from our collective unconscious that carries specific energy and can act upon the world? I had encountered the negative force of the collective unconscious long before I stumbled upon the works of Dr. Carl Gustav Jung who discovered this phenomenon. Dr. Jung saw that the collective unconscious influences the whole of the universe, and I am a witness to this truth.

I have lived in the United States since June of 1980 just as a silent witness to all the events that have unfolded in our world. I have never voiced out my thoughts about anything until something very strange started to manifest to me. I have admired people who get involved actively in social matters, but my shyness and meekness prevented me from doing anything. It is embarrassing to admit that it had to take a horrible deed of young students to prod me to speak out. The appalling deeds of these two young students turned killers finally gave me the courage to break out from my meekness and silence. I believe I know why these young students became killers. I believe I know what turns a person into a murderer.

It was a demonic force that came to me, which tortured me during the last three months of 1975. During those horrendous three months,

I fought with all my might against a force, which was compelling me to kill everyone around me whenever I saw a knife, or any sharp and pointed implement that can kill. I had to hold both my hands tightly behind my back to defy this powerful force that was compelling me to reach for the knives. I knew the compelling urge to kill was not mine. At the time I was experiencing this horrible ordeal, I knew I was fighting against a demonic force foreign from my own being, but I did not know that it was a force coming from the collective unconscious. Because of my Christian upbringing, I perceived the force to be Satan. I now know that Satan is the force created by our own collective unconscious. Satan is the collective force created by the thought energies of everyone who nurtures hatred and entertains destructive evil and perverse thoughts with desires of hurting, violating, and killing someone. My strong moral indoctrination from my youth with my sound mind and clear conscience free of any guilt of wrongdoing towards anyone gave me the full trust that God will never allow evil to overcome a good person like me, which enabled me to overcome this demonic force.

My encounter of this very powerful compelling dark force led me to understand what drove Richard Speck to commit his heinous multiple murders of those unfortunate nurses. Then there was Ted Bundy, the McDonald mass killer, the son of Sam, Jeffrey Dahmer, the Scotland mass killer of little children, Danny Rawlings, and many others. Each time the heinous deeds of morally weak men hit the news, a voice within me wanted me to cry out loud to humanity that I know what made these men kill. But alas! I could not break away from my meekness. I could not find the voice to tell the world about the force that tried to turn me into a murderer. But even if I did, how could I explain it? Who would believe me?

After Christmas of 1997, my new husband and I went to Mexico for our honeymoon. While we were in Merida, touring the sites of the ruins of Uxmal and Chitchen Itza, very powerful visions told me that the god that commanded Abraham to sacrifice his son as burnt offering written in Genesis 22;2 of the Bible, and the god who told the children of Israel to kill everything that breathes in the land of their inheritance written in Deuteronomy 20;16 of the Bible, was the same as the Mayan god demanding human sacrifice and the demonic force that tried to turn me into a senseless murderer in 1975. I was riveted where I stood when I suddenly came to the awareness that this intelligent presence communicating with me was God, the Supreme Power Above was talking to me! Through the Bible, the SPA (Supreme Power Above) revealed to me the true meanings of the parables and the true meanings of the words of Jesus.

I shared my experience with my science-oriented husband who had remained skeptical about my whole revelation, but it was he who suggested to me to look into the works of Dr. Carl Gustav Jung. I was greatly relieved and overjoyed to realize that Dr. Jung had already gained insight into what the SPA revealed to me. I did not possess the terminology needed to relay to others the knowledge that had been revealed to me, but through the works of Dr. Jung, I found the terminology to explain my newly found truth. The SPA confirmed the profoundness of Dr. Jung's theory of the collective unconscious!

Where are the Jungian advocates? Why have they not come forward to clarify the true nature and cause of the crimes that are being perpetrated in our generation? Is it because Dr. Jung was a Nazi who shared the anti-Semitic sentiments during the Second World War that his works are being ignored? Paul persecuted the Christians too, before God enlightened him. I see Dr. Jung as our modern version of Paul. God spoke to him as well. He thanked God that he had been permitted to experience the reality of the "Imago Dei" in him. Otherwise, he said that he would have been a bitter enemy of Christianity and the church. He said that the existence of God is an incontrovertible certainty. Did the Jungian advocates keep their silence because they themselves failed to comprehend the full significance of Dr. Carl Gustav Jung's discovery of the phenomenon of the collective unconscious? I would never have perceived this phenomenon on my own had the Supreme Power Above not given me visions that clearly showed me its mechanics.

I do not believe that gun control alone will solve the ills that are plaguing our present-day society because guns basically are harmless until someone pulls its trigger, and guns are not the only weapons for murder. I believe the solution lies in understanding the very root of it all. There is so much violence in our world, why?

The SPA revealed to me that in the parable of the seed and the Sower, life are the seeds, and the SPA is the Sower. Science has no explanation of how the very complex formulation of DNA came about but I saw very vivid visions of how we evolved from a simple celled microorganism into the intelligent beings that we are now. From the minute speck of energy that the SPA sowed on earth more than four billion years ago, we have evolved into the clever beings that we are now. But we are not yet clever enough to free our psyches completely of the remnants of our violent defense mechanism when we were still in a much lower animal state. What is happening is that instead of evolving into a higher state of being, we are allowing this violent animal psyche to pull as back, degenerating us back towards a state no different from lowly animals such as the dinosaurs which did not stop devouring each other until they all went extinct.

It is very alarming that our youths have lost their innocence, the innocence that would have been their shield from the satanic forces of the negative dynamic archetypes emanating from our collective unconscious. You reap what you sow, are we now reaping what we have sown? Are we now witnessing the effect of the subliminal messages that violent movies successfully conveyed to the minds of the corruptible, the subliminal message that life is cheap? The public has been entertained by violent movies that repeatedly portray how life is blasted off by a gun at the snap of a finger of a glorified mobster without any qualms. Movies depict how criminals get away from the law and enjoy the booties of their crimes. What kind of conscience are we instilling in the minds of our youths? Those kids who reenacted what they saw in the movies thought they were merely inflicting harmless flesh wounds, completely out of touch of reality. I agree that the media was only catering to the appetites of the masses that had relentlessly clamored for these violent movies. When are we going to wake up to all agree that this glorified violence portrayed over and over as a form of entertainment is damaging our collective unconscious? It is now damaging our general well-being in global proportions.

When are we going to wake up to see that the condition of our collective unconscious is already rotting from its core? How many more senseless murders are needed to wake us up? When are we going to realize that the kind of violent entertainment that we have patronized has been a big factor for the decadent state of our collective unconscious? Believe me, Dr. Carl Gustav Jung was very correct when he said that today too much is at stake and too much obviously depends upon the psychological qualities of man. I am making a plea to everyone, the only way to straighten up our collective unconscious is for us to turn back and believe in the words of God. We have a caring God who gave us the Ten Commandments to prevent us from creating the negative dynamic archetype that emanates from our collective unconscious. Let us all look into this phenomenon in the true light of social science and analytical psychology. Our own beliefs, fears, fantasies or daydreams, create a force that is either constructive or destructive. Let us turn away from materials that will continue to corrupt our collective unconscious.

The SPA has given us free will. All the SPA can do is to show us the way to evolve, but we must develop the decisiveness to get to that higher state of being on our own because that is the only way. That is the law of the universe. If we cannot develop the decisiveness to get to that higher state of being, then we do not deserve to get there. I heard a man say that if almighty powerful God exists, why doesn't He just eliminate all evil forces and be done with it? God will never do that because we are not puppets devoid of the ability to make decisions. God gave us the Commandments to prevent us from developing an evil collective force, but it is us who chose to create this demonic negative archetype in our collective unconscious. We made this mess; we must clean it up! Our planet Earth is a mere insignificant microscopic speck in the whole of our universe. God, the SPA does not need to prove anything to us. We must prove that we can reach the ultimate purpose of creation to reach that perfection that will enable us to metamorphose into pure energy to be one with God in eternal life as what Jesus accomplished. This is why Jesus said: Come follow me!

I am not the only one who witnessed the forces emanating from our collective unconscious. All the people who have claimed to have seen the apparition of Jesus and Mary the mother of Jesus, all the people who claimed to experience seeing a ghost or poltergeist or being abducted by aliens, and everyone who saw crop circles that were so geometrically complex are also witnesses to the manifestations of the forces of archetypes created by collective beliefs, fears and fantasies that emanate from our collective unconscious. Even the story of Joan of Arc is a testimony to this phenomenon, which was created by the collective beliefs in the legend of the maid of Lorraine who was to come to save them.

As Dr. Jung said, the archetype is a phenomenon of "God-like" dimensions. It is in a very real sense alive and functioning in the world. The archetypes have their own initiative and their own specific energy as what manifested to me. These powers enable them both to produce meaningful interpretation and to interfere in a given situation exactly as what I experienced.

We are all missing the true Christian message of love and peace. Look back in our history at how the Romans turned Jesus into a deity and created a Great War machine in the name of Christ. If one would look diligently in the original Bible, (not edited to conform with Christian belief system) one would find that Jesus said: "Do not worship me, worship God in heaven." Jesus said, "Follow even the least of my commandments", but Christians defied the words of Jesus and waged violent holy wars in his name, fulfilling the prophesy in the Book of Revelation of a violent god who would lead people in holy wars. There is never a holy war, there is only deadly war. Can you blame Dr. Jung for saying that the Christ and the Antichrist are one and the same? They are both forces emanating from our collective unconscious. How many lives have been lost fighting for the "Holy City"? There is no such thing as a Holy City, there is only deadly city.

Some people are looking for the Antichrist as a human. It is not human. It is a great evil spirit, which we created from collective false beliefs with God-like powers that can possess a human to commit heinous crimes, such as terrorists so proud of their abominable murders that they post live on the internet following their false prophet to smite the neck of infidels. Their false prophet blinded them to see that they are being led to violate the Commandment of God – DO NOT KILL! I am a firsthand witness to this because I fought against this horrible force and I am a witness to its formidable powers. I defied this evil force from reaching for murder weapons but when it physically held both my hands to strangle myself, my mortal strength was completely incapacitated. The SPA had to rescue me to free my hands because on my own, I had no power whatsoever, as if my arm was completely disconnected from my nervous system. It was a relief to realize that I was not the only one who experienced this evil attempt to kill myself with my own hands controlled by Satan, when I saw a documentary on TV about this horrendous phenomenon they call "Alien Hand Syndrome." I overcame it because I confronted it fearlessly unlike those shown on TV who were in complete terror that they developed the syndrome. Again, there is nothing to fear but fear itself. My clear conscience free of any guilt from any wrongdoing gave me complete trust in God's saving grace that enabled me to fight fearlessly.

Do you have the moral integrity to defy this force or discern it if it comes to you? Are we raising our children to be immune from this evil force? The crimes committed by these poor morally inadequate youths are testaments to their parents' failure. We have a long list of serial killers, spree killers. Are these not enough to convince us of the presence of the Anti-Christ? Andrew Cunanan baffled experts because his profile did not fit the profile of serial killers, and they were left puzzled. Is this not enough proof of how formidable the power of the Anti-Christ is?

It is now judgement day. Those who have succumbed to the seductions of the dark negative forces of the collective unconscious will be judged. The SPA gave me clear visions of what will happen to those who will suffer a second death, the death of their consciousness or soul after the death of they physical body to be permanently dead, no more thinking nor reasoning. I saw irredeemable souls, which is really our consciousness, turn into particles in the magma chamber of earth that oozes out as lava, written in the Bible as sinners souls cast to the lake of fire. The SPA showed me that this is the meaning of what science's Higgs-Boson findings of energy turning into a particle of matter. Geologists, you have the task of answering this question: where did the islands of Hawaii and Iceland come from? They are both Island groups that are not part of the original Pangea. The vision I saw of the residual energy of the irredeemable soul turning into lava particle is the opposite of splitting the atom to produce a bomb. A bomb is matter turned into energy, a sinner soul is turned into a particle of matter, which to me appears as the law of creation.

This brings to my mind the tale of the fall of Lucifer and his minions where they were cast out of heaven. Did I conceive of the thought that getting cast out of heaven, Lucifer and his minions lit the fuse of what science call the Big Bang that started this physical universe 13.8 billion years ago? Or is this another truth revealed to me by the SPA? The SPA showed me that the seeds of life was sown on this physical universe with the ultimate purpose of turning matter back to pure energy to get back to heaven, the alternate universe, as what Jesus accomplished. Did you ever wonder why all ancient religions are mostly human sacrificing religions? Was this the work of Lucifer to maintain this physical universe which he is pursuing to completely dominate? Did he started religions with gods demanding human sacrifice to keep those creatures that evolved to possess intelligence, earthbound, preventing them from attaining the ultimate purpose of life to turn into pure energy to be one with God in eternal life in heaven? Lucifer is anti-life because life turns matter into energy, so he wants all humans to be evil to prevent them from going back to the alternate universe we call heaven. He continuously feeds human minds with evil suggestions so that they will all be cast to the lake of fire to burn there until they become the dirt of the earth, dead forever. Satan is his general who continuously possess the morally bankrupt and mentally impaired to commit murders to kill them permanently body and soul. Science has no explanation why our universe is continuously expanding, The SPA showed me that as intelligent beings from all over our universe reach the perfection of Jesus and metamorphose into pure energy or rapture in Christian terminology or reach Nirvana in Buddhist terminology, so does our universe expands.

I overcame Satan's power of suggestions which felt like I was responsible for the evil thought but since I never entertained evil thoughts, I realized how Satan can take over one's thinking process and possess the weaklings. I completely understand the power of Satan's suggestion feeding the Jews and Moslems with thoughts of animosity towards each other to keep them killing one another until they are all cast to the lake of fire. These thoughts of animosity toward each other do not allow them to remember that they are both descendants of Abraham. The Jews are children of Isaac, the Muslims children of Ismael. Both Isaac and Ysmael were sons of Abraham. Muslims are keeping alive the god of Balaam who appeared to Abraham and tried to turn Abraham's religion into a human sacrificing religion, This false god failed with the Jews and Christians but with the help of the false prophet of the god requiring human sacrifice who is the god of Balaam and the Mayans, (Lucifer in disguise) he was successful with Islam. Today's human sacrifice are suicide bombers, Muhammad Atta and his crew who attacked New York in 2001, and many others hailed by Muslims as martyrs, but the SPA showed me that they are now burning in the lake of fire and all their victims are now born again unto glorious new lives, reincarnated, as Jesus said, "You need to be born again to reach the kingdom of heaven".

You Jews and Muslims, open your eyes to this truth, you are brothers. Forgive each other and let bygones be bygones and start loving each other as true brothers so that true peace on earth will finally come. Jesus said – Beware of the false prophet dressed in sheep's clothing but is a ravenous wolf - who poisoned the hearts of the children of Ismael to hate their brothers, the children of Isaac. This false prophet brain washed his followers to love death because their god is the god of the dead as particles of physical matters devoid of any life dead forever. God is the God of the living and not of the dead, Matthew 22;31. No one has ascended to heaven (from Earth) except he who came down from heaven, John 3;13. Revelation 21;4 and death shall be no more. When we reach the ultimate purpose of life, we metamorphose body and soul into pure energy to be one with God in eternal life in heaven, no more lifeless cadavers are left behind, as what Jesus accomplished. Jesus did not die. There is a blood flow at the back waist of Jesus from his chest wound that was possible to happen because he turned to his side, meaning, he was alive when he raptured! Alleluia!

Each one of us will be tested. I passed my test when it came to me and I was rewarded with the privilege of having communion with the SPA. I am confident that I will pass another test if it comes again. Have you been tested yet? Did you pass your test when it came, or will you pass it when it comes? Those of you who failed the test and committed abominable crimes, your only chance of avoiding the burning inferno that awaits your soul when your physical body dies is to atone for your sins and sincerely repent for your evil deeds. There is no crime that goes unpunished. You are completely mistaken to think you have committed a perfect murder, because your victim's consciousness is not dead and it will be born again unto a glorious new life whereas, you murderer, your consciousness or soul shall be cast to the lake of fire to burn until you are the dirt of the earth dead forever. With admission of your guilt to lessen the grief of the loved ones of your victims and sincere repentance, you have a chance for redemption, but you will be born again in hell right here on earth, at least you are still alive. You have the choice to continue your evil ways towards your permanent demise to be the dirt of the earth, dead forever or be ready to accept going through a life of hardship in hell on earth to redeem yourself to be given a chance to be born again. We all need to be born again until we reach that perfection when we can be with the SPA in the highest level of existence possible. Protestants preach that you do not need to be perfect because the blood of Jesus saved you already, which is blasphemy. Jesus said – you need to be perfect as God in heaven is perfect, Matthew 5:48.

The public pays attention to people of ill repute for their notoriety. Would I qualify for a kind of notoriety worthy of the attention of the masses if I claim that I am the emissary of the second coming of Jesus so that I would get everyone's attention to listen to what I am saying? If this is the only way I could make everyone listen, then I am telling you that I am God's chosen emissary to bring to you the true meanings of the words of Jesus. I have seen God and He revealed to me all the secrets of the Bible, fulfilling Daniel 2:22 He reveals deep and hidden things. The SPA told me of the duality of the Bible; thus, the Bible is a two-edged sword. It has the power to enlighten and to deceive. I am writing my story with the title – *The Book of Life*. Please understand that I am not a writer, but the SPA bade me to share to the world what was revealed to me.

Matthew wrote twice in the Bible that a wicked and adulterous generation seeketh for a sign and the only sign given to it is the sign of Jonah. Jesus told me that I am Jonah. The dragon swallowed me and for three months I was in his belly unable to function normally. Armed with nothing but a little book entitled *The Imitation of Christ*, which I have followed diligently in my youth, I overcame the evil power of the dragon who could not digest me in his belly, so he spat me out, back to my freedom to bear witness to these truths I am sharing with you. Jesus told me that I am the queen from the south who rose up in the judgement with this generation and shall condemn it, for she came from the uttermost part of the Earth. The judgement is not mine; I am merely the messenger of the SPA to bring to Earth the truth, but indeed I had come from the uttermost part of the Earth, the Philippines, which is on the other side of the globe from where Jesus walked on earth. The Book of Revelation of the Bible tells of a strong angel with a little book. Jesus told me that I am the strong angel who overcame the dragon, and the little book is *The Imitation of Christ*, which contents I had fully digested that my life had been influenced by its guiding force. Jesus told me that I am he who had overcome as he had overcome, and I was given the white stone that bears a new name. On the beach, I found this white stone with letters SPA inscribed in it created by tiny organisms. SPA is for Supreme Power Above.

I asked the SPA to prove to mankind that I am truly His chosen emissary. He told me that I have the sign of the times. Suddenly, an outpouring of events in my life came surging into my mind, events that I wasn't aware of having any significance. The repeated pattern of the second number surged in my mind one after the other. I am the second child, the second daughter, I was born on the second hour of the second day of the second month while the Second World War was raging. My mother was born when all of Christendom was celebrating the birth of Jesus on December 25, 1922, and my year of birth was 22 years later, in 1944. Many major events of my life happened on the second or twenty second dates. I had no plan whatsoever to immigrate to the United States, but fate led me to come to this great nation in 1980, two decades before the end of the twentieth century. The SPA spoke to me twice, the first time was during my sign of Jonah ordeal in the last three months of 1975. Even 1975 is 1+9+7+5=22. The second time the SPA spoke to me was exactly 22 years later at the end of 1997, 2 years before the end of the 20th century. At that time, I was assigned workstation 2 at the Architectural office where I was employed and even my quick dial telephone code was number 22. These numbers came to me purely by chance. I joined a community choir unaware that I passed the audition to qualify on its 22nd season. Our Choir director deemed my voice to be soprano 2 and I was given the music folder 112. The closest major thoroughfare to my new residence when I moved to my new husband's residence is a state road that ends in number 22 and the exit from the highway that we frequently take is exit 22.

Many more repeated pattern of the second number followed me in my entire life. Both Jesus and Buddha have been portrayed with two fingers raised in sign of peace, were they both saying, watch out for the twos? My name Pura Regalado in English translates to Pure Gift. Even the names of all my sisters are related to Jesus. My older sister is Milagros, miracles. My younger sister is Anita, diminutive for Ann the grandmother of Jesus, mother of Mary. My youngest sister is Elizabeth, the cousin of Mary, mother of John. Are these synchronicities in my life meaningless coincidences or are these the SPA's sign of his power? Is this not enough to prove to us that even if our planet is so insignificantly microscopic viewing the entire universe, the most Supreme Power from Above cares for us?

Please do not judge me without a trial. I am a perfectly normal, sane, law-abiding citizen of the earth who singlehandedly raised three successful, intelligent, beautiful, happy children. Everyone who knows me, everyone I worked with will attest to the fact that I am free of any psychosis. Please do not dismiss me as someone who is having delusions because the SPA is my witness to my honesty. I have truly seen the SPA and He truly spoke to me. He wants us all to unify our beliefs so that peace on earth will finally come. He wants all differences in belief systems caused by manifestations of archetypes created by false beliefs that emanated from our collective unconscious be eradicated completely. The SPA sent one whose name is an adjective to describe the unified belief system which is the Pure Faith, no more belief systems that violates the 1st Commandment that forbids worship of any image from heaven earth or seas; no more belief systems that take God's name in vain by believing in false gods that tell people to kill which are in fact manifestations of archetypes created by false beliefs, no more killings and wars and Earth shall be Paradise where every moment is joyful!

CHAPTER 2

THE BOOK OF LIFE

Hello, people of the world! I, Pura Regalado, an Architect from the Philippines and a naturalized American citizen who has been a permanent residence of the United States since 1980, do hereby solemnly swear that I have seen the true God who is the Supreme Power Above. I have witnessed the Second Coming of Jesus. He who has an ear listen to what the Supreme Power from Above bade me to say.

The Supreme Power Above led me to discover for myself that man's beliefs, fantasies, fears, all kinds of thoughts in the collective, create compelling forces that affect our society, and it is my task to convey to you these truths that were revealed to me. God has shown me science and religion reconciled. Ever since I graduated from college to become an Architect in 1966, I have chosen to be a mere observer of events that unfold year after year in our world. I very seldom express my own opinion about anything, I have become the silent witness who in my own way had evaluated the causes and effects of man's behavior that shaped the condition of the world that we live in today. Never had I imagined that the day would come when a task of this great magnitude would be bestowed upon me. I am aware that what I have to say may cause the renting of clothes and gnashing of teeth by those who believe themselves experts of the Bible and experts on all matters about God because the truth revealed to me is far from any interpretations I have heard from any proclaimed Bible expert.

Dr. Carl Gustav Jung had seen the Antichrist. I had wrestled against this Antichrist. The antichrist is leading our species to extinction. The only chance of our species' survival depends on our full-hearted willingness to come together as one big, united force to eliminate this Antichrist. Christ came to our world two thousand years ago to save us from extinction. He was just not the Messiah for the children of Israel or for the children of Ismael, He did not come to save just a few tribes against one another. He is the messiah of every man on earth today as we come to face the final judgement of our species. He knew it will take two millennia before His true message would be truly understood by someone who could reach Him, someone who could bring His words back to light to help us survive a coming cataclysm that is threatening to annihilate all of us. I was given the key to open the bottomless pit where the Antichrist can be cast to perdition, but all I can do is to open it. The collective force of every man on earth is needed to do the big task of eliminating the Antichrist for good. God has given us free will. It is up to us to choose whether we eliminate the Antichrist or not. The survival of our species depends on our decision. Everything I have written truly happened, there is no truthful person on earth who will testify otherwise. The true God is my witness to my honesty. If my story cannot convince you or if after reading my story you still cannot believe that there is God, then I challenge you to explain all the synchronicities in my life and the phenomena that happened to me. Even in murder investigations, when there are too many coincidences, the ensuing conclusion is premeditated murder.

I am not a writer; I have never written any kind of story before in my life because I am an Architect trained to express my ideas in design graphically and I never expected that I would have this task to write about something I experienced. I have not even written to any of my beloved relatives in the Philippines since I came to the United States before I started this story. Every time I needed to reach any of them, I chose to use the telephone so that I could hear their voices. This is the first time ever that I have written about something I have experienced because the true God gave me the task to share with you what He revealed to me. I remember though that when I was in high school, our English teacher always gave me extra research homework, which was not given to any of my other classmates. Was it to keep me from boredom because I was always the top-ranking English student? I do not possess any talent for writing and the proper words to convey what I wanted to say did not come easily to me because English is my second language, next to Tagalog, my native language that I was brought up with. But I will try to make everything as clear as I can. Where to begin my story was the first dilemma that confronted me, but I thought you would understand me better if I gave you a brief history of my life that led me to reach the SPA.

Since my youth I have always searched for the purpose of my life. I remember being so frustrated by the uselessness of my life when I was a young woman in college preparing to become an Architect. Although I always ranked top in class, I was never satisfied with my performance and I always thought that I could have done better. I was such a perfectionist that I was always driven to give my best performance whenever I tackled anything, although self-glory was not what motivated me but the challenge to do the best I could in whatever I did. My little book taught me to put myself last, so I never sought anything for myself so that aspiring for a career seemed meaningless even when I was doing well in school. I kept telling God, "You can take me anytime you want, I see no purpose for my life at all."

My sister Elizabeth who was a student at a Catholic elementary school asked me to make a hand drawn greeting card for her teacher who was a nun. She must have liked the handmade greeting card I made, and she requested me to make more for her. I met her one time when I picked up Elizabeth after her classes were over. She was such a jolly nun who was merrily jumping in glee when she saw the handmade greeting cards I made for her. I thought I would be a happy num like her devoted to spirituality and nothing else. I was in the third year of my Architecture course when I told my mother that I would not want to continue studying to be an Architect. I wanted to be a nun instead. My mother told me, "Pura, you are my second child. Heaven forbids something happens to your Apang (that's how my siblings and I called our beloved father), I might need your help bringing up your six siblings after to you." Mama gave me the perfect answer that woke me up. Had she objected of me becoming a nun for reasons benefitting me alone, I would have gone straight to the nunnery. She was right,

I was being selfish thinking only of what I wanted so I continued my Architectural studies, and I was the only scholar of the graduating class of 1966.

Bert, a schoolmate from the Chemical Engineering department started showing me attention and to take my mind off the nunnery, I entertained his attention and two years after graduating from college we got married. He turned out to be a sick man who needed a major surgery, a lobectomy to cut off the infected lowest lobe of his right lung and the middle lobe that was starting to be infected was saved by a process they call decortication. My first year of marriage was spent on bringing my husband back to health, which I managed to singlehandedly cope with financially, emotionally and physically. Taking care of my sick husband gave purpose for my life. When his health was restored, we had three children and motherhood gave me the purpose in life that I searched for and my prayers changed to, "Please God, don't take me yet until my youngest one is at least twenty years old."

Years went by so quickly; the first years of my married life were full of ordeals to overcome specially when my husband satisfied his need for another woman who can give him that macho image that he couldn't feel with me after being under my care while he was sick. However, a time came when I thought my marital problem was over when he started bringing home books of Ruth Montgomery about automatic writing and he told me that he was searching for the truth. Alas! Ruth Montgomery's suggestions of invoking spirits was the bait that led me to the jaws of the dragon that swallowed me alive to start the agony of my sign of Jonah ordeal which I managed to overcome through Gods' saving grace. This harrowing ordeal gave my husband the excuse to abandon me and my children in 1978. My oldest son was only eight years old at that time. With the help of my little book, I survived it all. If Jesus carried his cross, who am I not to carry mine?

Somehow, I managed to single-handedly bring up my three young ones. My children, whom I love so dearly, became the major force that kept me pushing to survive. They gave me the purpose for which my life became worthwhile. One by one they went to college and started to have lives of their own. When my youngest one left for college, I found myself back to square one. I did not have a purpose for my life again. The empty nest syndrome, magnified by the fact that I did not have a partner intensified the uselessness of my life that drove me to a severe depression. However, after many years of hardships, my survival instinct had hardened, and I managed to find the strength to snap out of my depression to get going with my life. I knew that life had to go on at whatever cost. Cutting my life short with my own hands was never an option. I can never disobey God's law.

I owe my survival to my little book – *The Imitation of Christ* - that had been my guide since I was sixteen years old. Following the philosophy of life laid out by Jesus helped me manage to keep my stresses down to minimum most of the time. Some think that the teaching set forth by Jesus is humanly impossible to follow, but I was ready to face the challenge. Contrary to what others think, I found the teachings set forth by Jesus not really a challenge but more of a lever that lightened the weight of my burdens. Jesus is my friend and mentor who carried his cross until the end, so I took all the miseries of my life as my own crosses, which I patiently bore until the pain ceased to hurt. When Bert turned his back on me and my children, I was cast into an ocean of fear as to how I would raise my children to be emotionally stable without a father, which gave tremendous pain in my heart. It hurt so badly but I knew I had to survive for my children's sake. I knew time would heal anything. The only question was when? How long would it take till it hurts no more?

Jesus said that if someone slaps me on my cheek, I should let my other cheek be slapped as well, so that was exactly what I did. I returned kindness and generosity for the cruelty of others. I was severely emotionally and physically abused by Bert before he left me, but when he needed a new car, he came to me for financial help. I made a loan of five thousand pesos to help him buy his brand-new car even if I knew his passenger would be his concubine. There were also times when he came asking me for money, which I did not hesitate to give even when we were already separated. He never paid me back, but I feel no bitterness towards him because my little book taught me to have a forgiving heart.

All my friends dissuaded me from jumping into marriage, a major decision of my life. "You are going to ruin your future", they all said.

"There are a lot of men out there who can make you happy. Why will you burden yourself with this sick man?" they all asked me. I did not listen to any of them, How could I turn my back to a man who needed help? I went ahead and married Bert against the advice of everyone who cared for me, no wedding gown, no marching down the aisle, not even a proper wedding ring, I borrowed Mama's ring for the ceremony when we said our I dos at the wedding rites conducted by Father Robles at the Mt. Carmel Catholic church. I made all the arrangements to get him treated at Quezon Institute hospital in Manila that specialized in lung ailments. The medical staff at QI were so considerate and sympathetic they made Bert's major surgery affordable for me. I moved to a newly constructed apartment close to my parents' home. Bert came home with me to our new apartment when he was released from QI to continue his convalescence in our new home. The first year of my married life was a real challenge.

A month before I had my first baby, Bert had fully recuperated from his surgery and started working at a tobacco company. On the day I started feeling labor pains and I needed to go to the hospital to have my baby, he could not be found. Mama and my cousin Nympha were the ones who took me to the hospital. Later on, I was shocked to be told that it was because he had found a new lover as soon as he had started his employment. It felt like Heaven and Earth closed in on me. I could not believe Bert could ever do what he had done right after he got well! Oh, sweet Jesus! You know men so well when you said not to expect anything from them because they are ungrateful wretches. All the years I spent with Bert were very turbulent years, but I never upbraided him with what I had done for him. On that day that he brutally abused me physically, all I could say was, "This is what I get for taking care of you at the hospital". He screamed back at me with, "Are you God?" A month after that incident, he finally decided to abandon me and my three children. I was so broken-hearted but not for my own sake. I would have been better off without him but my concern were for our children, how would they grow up without a father? I begged him to stay, "You don't have to be a husband for me, but please stay and be a father to our children." Alas, Bert has a heart of stone.

I raised my two sons and my only daughter without any child support from Bert. It was not for me to demand from him his responsibilities to our children. A responsible man would do his duty without being asked. Since I did not ask for his support, he did not give it. He came to visit the children with his new wife sixteen years later at a time when I was going through a severe depression. It was then that I could not stop myself from expressing my anger at what he had done even over the objection of my children, whom I raised loving their father no matter what because God commanded to honor your father and mother. My sense of righteousness compelled me to express my disgust at what he had done to let him know he was wrong. I needed to do it to hasten my healing within. Although I had already forgiven him long before, I knew my healing would be complete only after I could confront him with his misgivings. I don't think I will ever stop caring for him. What I feel for him is just like what I feel for my children. When he turned fifty, he suddenly started to know his children better. He started to help my youngest son in college and invited all three to visit him up in New Jersey where he had been a resident since 1982. It took a tremendous amount of persuasion from me before my oldest son obliged, I told him. "It's your chance to see New York for free!" He agreed.

I did not have any desire to migrate to America. I was among those Filipinos who were concerned that the Philippines was getting brain-drained because many professionals were leaving the country to look for greener pastures abroad. It seems to me that tribalism in the Philippines has not been eradicated by foreign colonization. Until now, tribalism is a big factor in elections of officials in the seat of government. Filipino voters do not consider what will be the best for the whole nation, they vote for what's best for their tribes or what's best for their personal interest not for the whole nation. Elections in the Philippines are popularity contests, the most popular candidate, usually a movie star, win elections, not because he is the best to govern the country but because he was a popular celebrity. It seems that all former colonies of Spain never developed patriotism in their own birth of place, majority seek for greener pastures usually in America to flee the corruptions in their own country, corruptions that are deeply rooted because under the colonization of Spain, the mainland sent officials to their colonies who were being punished for their corruptions, to be the governadorcillos of their colonies. America, under an open border policy, you are condoning the corruptions in the countries where undocumented immigrants are coming from, aren't you concerned that under an open border policy, the USA will be overpopulated such that the land to grow food will be insufficient to feed all?

In 1974, there was a shortage of nurses in the United States. An American recruiting agency came to the Philippines and my sister Anita, six years younger than me, had just graduated from the University of the Philippines school of Nursing and was recruited to work in hospitals in the US together with nine other co-graduates of her. After working for four years, she was granted an immigrant status, then got married to a very nice young man and settled in Florida. Mama and Apang, followed Anita to the US after Anita's short visit that summer to meet her husband. Our parents came back home announcing that Anita was going to have a baby! Mama could not imagine her beloved daughter having a baby in a place where she did not have any close relative. She persuaded me to go to America to be with my sister when her baby was born. I somehow suspected that Mama was pushing me to go to America for a hidden reason; was she pushing me to go to a country where there is divorce? Divorce is not allowed under Philippine laws. Even if Bert was already living with another woman, his concubine, making them both guilty of concubinage punishable with imprisonment under Philippine law, I was not free to have a relationship with another man, otherwise, I will be guilty of adultery, which is disdained by Filipino morality.

Getting a visitor's visa to go to the United States is not at all easy, but I could not let Mama down. I am a person who is like that Tevye character in *Fiddler on the Roof* who always talks to God when he is alone. I told God, "I will try to get a visa but once. If you like me to go to America, then I shall get a visa on my first try because I will not try it again." God wanted me to go to America. I got my one-year visa on my first try and in June 1, 1980, I was on a plane bound for Fort Lauderdale, Florida. Six weeks later, the baby who brought me to America was born and she was baptized with the name Nicole.

In the United States, I applied for a divorce from Bert. Although the Philippine laws do not allow divorce, it respects US laws. I met a man whom I shall call Nick. Being a Catholic, I felt that I was taking the path towards violating God's law: Do not commit adultery. I told God, "if I will offend you by being with another man, then don't let anything happen between Nick and me." It looks like God gave me his permission because Nick and I got married in 1981 and my visitor's visa became an immigrant visa. Nick was involved in building construction, and he recommended me to Architect Allan Kozich in Fort Lauderdale, my first employer in USA. Because of Nick, an American citizen being the petitioner of my three underage children, who automatically became his adopted children, my three little ones came to join me in this great USA in May of 1983. They had to wait for the Philippine school year of 1982-83 to end before they came to join me.

Nick put his best foot forward when he met me, but his true colors appeared when my three children, who were at their playful, rumbunctious stage running all over Nick's apartment, was added to our household. I was employed at that time by the land developer MAP Builders who built several condominium complexes in the city of Coral Springs. I fortunately got one three-bedroom apartment unit despite all units getting sold out before the construction started because one of the buyers failed to acquire a housing loan. It was a time when condominiums in Florida were in demand.

Nick's condominium was an adult community for ages 55 and above but his youngest son Jim was living with him. We moved to my brand-new apartment which I bought without Nick's help and 18-year-old Jim was left at his condo apartment. Since I was an employee of MAP Builders, I was granted a $5,000 discount by the company. Nick lived with me and my children without offering to contribute to our finances. My American husband did not offer to help, and I was not one to ask. If he had been a fair man, he should have volunteered. I was not aware of the ways of Americans at that time, and I had wondered if that was the American way. In fact, my American husband made me feel that he did not have any intention of investing anything in our marriage after my children had come to join us. He offered not a penny, nor did he offer any piece of furniture that he already owned to furnish our brand-new apartment. We opened a joint bank account from my personal income, but he never deposited anything to it, not even a penny. His income was all set aside for his gambling addiction which he hid from me before we got married. He had connections with all the bookies in Florida where he put his bet and each time he lost his bet, he released his frustrations in me with all sorts of verbal abuse. He was also a very domineering man who controlled everything I did. I got lashed with ugly crude profanity when I bought an Omni magazine and when I did some clothes shopping with my children. I was spending my own hard-earned money, why? Since then, every time we went out shopping, I asked my son to go in our apartment first to open the bedroom window to smuggle all our shopping items into our apartment without Nick seeing them.

I have never uttered any kind of profanity in my life, and I was raised in a family of sweet loving people. It was so revolting that I had to take this unkind treatment, but I did not want any argument. I learned to bite my tongue and let his ugly words go in one ear and out the other. I also saw physical evidence of his adultery, but I dreaded the thought of another divorce. I was scared of the idea of not having a man in the house in a strange new land, so I took all his abuse and continued to perform what was expected from a wife the best way I could. He had freshly cooked dinner every night.

Nick tried to leave me one time and joined his son Jim at his Deerfield Beach apartment. The instant big family with three young playful children was too much for him. After a week, he came back with the excuse that he lost his temper because my apartment was too crowded for five of us, and he suggested that we build a bigger house. I designed the house and since I was working with the developer MAP Builders, I was in contact with all the subcontractors that we needed to build our new home. Nick purchased a lake-front lot in Coral Springs that at that time only cost $30 thousand and we started the construction of our new home from whatever savings I had. The rest of the house was built slowly out of whatever he made every month while I single-handedly supported our household. Our new house was completed without any mortgage.

Nick's tension mounted as the construction of the house progressed and his verbal abuses became more relentless. I knew it was because of the money he was investing in our new house. He must have been paranoid of the fact I was legally entitled to half of the cost of the house we were building that made him go berserk. The verbal abuse led to physical abuse just before we could move into our newly constructed house that was already approved for occupancy.

We were just finishing supper one evening when he got a call from his bookie telling him that he lost his bet on a game. He got so furious, grabbed both of my arms as I sat on a chair by the dining table finishing my supper and flung my 94-pound small body down to the floor. He raised his foot to step on my face. I quickly turned my face to the side and the sole of his shoe landed on my cheek. I saw the beastly look on his face as the dirty sole of his shoe pressed on my cheek. It was a great relief that he came to his senses before he could crack my skull. As I lay helpless on the cold floor, my thoughts were on my children. If this evil man should kill me, who would take care of my little ones who are all so helplessly dependent on me? I started asking myself why I had to put up with all the abuses of this cruel man. When I married him, I saw in his previous divorce document that his ex-wife divorced him for cruelty, but he denied it saying that it was the excuse of his adulterous ex-wife. He was not even helping me in any way, he was a freeloader in my household by all definitions. I put up with all his abuses believing that he would protect me and my children in case there was an attacker. Now that this person whom I depended on for protection had become my attacker, I knew I had to put an end to it.

As soon as I got up on my feet, I dialed 911, I summoned the police to come and send him out of our apartment. The Police officers told me that I needed a court order to get my husband out. This cruel man vehemently denied his beastly actions to the police, accusing me of being the conniving liar. He even found the audacity to say to the officers that God would take care of the liar. The indignity was too much to bear, and I felt so unjustly treated and more helpless than ever when the police officers left.

Anyway, God immediately took care of the liar. After work the following day, he came home limping, his ankle broken and his face grimacing with pain. I asked him if it was the same foot with which he stepped on me, and he nodded in reply without saying a word. He knew he better not tell a lie again. I told him, "You said, God will take care of the liar. Well, He did." Although I wanted him out of my sight, his pitiful condition aroused my compassion. I brought him supper in bed that night and the following morning, before I left for work, I told my twelve-year-old daughter, "There is a sick man in our home; give him breakfast."

I refused to sleep in our bedroom from that evening when he cruelly stepped on my face, and I slept in our living room couch until I got the court order that forced him to get out of my apartment. He was ordered not to come within a fifty feet radius wherever I was. The judge did not have any hesitation in coming up with this judgment because the whole event was witnessed by my youngest son who testified for me. Although he was instructed by the court to take nothing but his clothes, he took with him my drafting board, my sewing machine and everything he had given me as birthday presents for the four years we were married. It was the first time my check to pay the mortgage of my condo apartment bounced because he also took out $8,000 from the bank account I opened joint with him which was all my hard-earned money since he never contributed a penny to it. He forcefully grabbed my key chain from my hand to get my car key and drove away with my car, which I bought with my hard-earned money without his help. I had to walk over a mile to work until I managed to buy another car.

Why God sent me these heartless men I did not know. I know that each time I overcame a big storm in my life, I became a stronger person, and I know that I did turn my other cheek when they slapped me as Jesus bade me to do in my little book. In fact, both these men got away with nice four-bedrooms houses, which I designed and built, and I did not get a penny for my professional service as the Architect and builder for these two beautiful homes. Nick told me that he had connections with the Mafia, and he can make a murder look like an accident. I knew it was a threat to frighten me from claiming my rights for half of the value of our newly built home.

I couldn't take the risk of getting murdered and orphan my three young children in this foreign land, so I signed off everything to him, but I made sure that all the sub-contractors for the construction of our house were paid in full before I signed our divorce agreement. The air conditioning contractor Carl Lindstrom gave me the assurance that he trusted that Nick would be good to him, and he told me not to worry about it. A few months later, he told me that Nick still owed him $5,000, I told him, I'm sorry, I already signed off everything to him, you told me not to worry about it. Nick could easily sell our house for $130,000 in 1985 which by today's economy would easily fetch half a million dollars. I don't know what Bert did to the house I designed and built back in the Philippines. I did not fight for material things that were rightfully mine because I did not want to prolong the emotional aggravations that go with divorce proceedings, a righteous man would have given me my share voluntarily.

After a couple of years, Nick tried to win me back with the promise of building another house. I am such a soft-hearted being that I might have forgiven him and accepted him back knowing how truly cruel and evil he was. However, my daughter told me that before our divorce, she was about 12 years old at that time, Nick grabbed her butt while she was washing dishes after our supper. My daughter had blossomed into a beautiful teenager and there was no way I could endanger her purity in the hands of this monster. While he knelt before me with his offer, I did not say a word, I merely looked at him straight in his eyes. He then in resignation said, "I must have been a real a,,hole" (I've never spoken a vulgar word in my life and I wouldn't start by quoting him). He left and he must have made up unsavory stories about me that our neighbor in his condo in Deerfield Beach, looked at me with disdain when I met her by chance. All I can do is forgive as what Jesus said, which saved myself from emotional aggravations that would have aged me three times faster. For me, to attain peace of mind the quickest possible was worth all the money or material things I could have gotten if I chose to fight for what was rightfully mine.

Come to think about it, my little book was also the reason why I felt that my life was without any purpose. It taught me to be selfless. That was why I never fought for anything material for myself. When there is no self to think of, then what is the purpose of pursuing a career or self-gratification? On the other hand, when you are selfless, you can tolerate the misgivings of others because there is no self to get hurt, so you avoid getting stressed out by obnoxious behaviors of others. Truly, the words of Jesus are in fact, stress management.

Envy was something that used to bother me when I was a little girl. I used to envy my older sister Mila for getting all the new clothes, while I only got the hand-me-downs that she had outgrown. I did not understand that right after the war, my father's earnings were not enough to afford to buy us both new clothes and anyway, Mila outgrew her clothes before they were worn out. But I learned very young that I did not want to be miserable because of envy. I learned to accept the way things were, and I learned to appreciate the meager things I had, so the virtue of selflessness was easy for me to adopt. In fact, it is an effective suppressant for desiring material things, which I could not afford anyway because I did not have the money to spend in the first place. Selflessness freed me from want. If one is selfless, he or she will never care if others have better things than he or she has. The worth of material things anyway depends on one's value judgement. What is valuable to one may be worthless to another.

I had quite an exciting childhood. I had a very loving family. Apang, my father had a legacy of generosity that had permeated the lives of all his children. Although we were poor, we always had enough. My young life was not devoid of little mysterious happenings either. I had been sensing a sort of whisper in the wind since I was a little girl. Sometimes, it was calling my name affectionately, sometimes telling me that it loves me or making me feel that I was sort of a special person. I would turn around, look everywhere to see where the sound came from, only to find that it came from nowhere. My cousin Estring, Apang's niece, who joined our household before I was a teenager, said one time that if I heard anything like that, don't answer, just let it be. I was comforted to know that I was not the only one having that kind of experience. This sort of talking wind came to me perhaps once a year when I was little but as I got older, it gradually came more often, and I got used to it and learned to ignore it. *It's my mind playing tricks on me*, I would tell myself.

My teenage years were the rock and roll era and like any other teenager, Mila and I were in a rock and roll jam session every week. Jesus said not to worry what to wear, and I never did. At fourteen, I got tired of hand-me-down clothes from Mila. I started sewing at a very young age, making ragdolls, and at age fourteen, I was an expert dressmaker able to draft my own patterns and design my own clothes. I went to a vocational high school that had a dressmaking class, and

I always produced the best project and that's how I learned to sew, crochet or knit dresses. I saved my allowance to buy the fabrics, which I sewed into pretty party dresses. Every time I went to a party, I wore a brand-new pretty party dress, and I bet no one knew that I spent very much less than what the other girls spent on their dresses, and yet my dress was just as pretty as theirs. Being in a household that operated on a very tight budget was constructive for me. It prodded me to develop my many talents. When I needed a picture to hang on my wall, I painted it myself because the kind of wall hangings that appealed to my taste were too expensive for my pocket. I had learned to draw very early. It looks like I was born with the talent. I was the winner of an art competition for all grade schoolers of Manila when I was ten years old. My drawing entry was the portrait of Elizabeth Taylor with crayons as my medium and I titled it – My Favorite Actress.

My name was something I used to be ashamed of when I was little. I thought it did not sound nice for a girl. Why didn't Mama name me Helen, or Maria? They sound so feminine; I used to think. Then, at the start of 1950, Mama came home with a Catholic calendar. I was such a precocious child, and this calendar instantly became the object of my curiosity. Each day of this calendar indicated a feast day of a saint or a celebration of an event. The picture of the honored saint or a symbol of an event was also illustrated on each box for each day. It was a very pleasant surprise for me when I found out that my birthday, the second day of February, was the Purification Day of the Blessed Virgin Mary. Mama told me that was how I got my name. Purification was shortened to Pura, meaning pure. I finally learned to like my name after that. However, my young inquisitive mind was deeply puzzled by one thing: how did the people who made the calendar know that blessed Mary was purified on the second day of February? Did they make it up or did God tell them it was so? Anyway, since my name means pure, I decided to be pure for my name's sake until I met the man I married.

Because I wanted to be pure, getting romantically involved with any man was something I avoided like a plague while I was a student. Getting a college diploma was my goal and romantic involvement, aside from endangering my purity, would be a distraction. I avoided anything that would take my mind off my studies. Boys were just friends. I had a platonic sidekick named Danny while I was in high school, and that was the closest attachment I could have with boys.

I did allow myself to have crushes on men who showed skills comparable to mine. When I got to college I was always ranked first in class, I was elected class president every year. My first crush was Rick, who was two years ahead of me. I was a sophomore, and he was a senior, academically top of the class, who probably thought of me as a mere kid. When he started dating someone, my heart was crushed. After Rick graduated. My attention went to Gene (a classmate whose capabilities were close to mine) who accompanied me home one evening after school, which was promising, but not having any experience in the dating game, I must have wrongfully given him the signal that I was not interested, so he diverted his attention to someone else. After that, no one from the Architectural department of MIT Philippines asked me out for a date and I heard one of them say, "How can I ask someone smarter than me for a date?" He was right, I cannot accept one whose capabilities cannot surpass or at least equal mine. That was me in the early sixties, the virgin who made a vow of chastity until I met the man I would marry, which is typical trait of Filipino women. At that time, our contemporaries in America were probably either getting carefully indoctrinated with the meaning of the Bible by theology experts or rallying for the sexual revolution.

Jesus said that if my eyes should cause me to sin, I should pluck them out. Oh no, I would never want to go blind, so I never entertained evil or perverse thoughts. My mind was never idle anyway. My many talents had kept my mind awfully busy. I always had so many projects planned that my mind was constantly busy designing and calculating how to carry out my projects. On a bus on my way to school, my mind was either pondering lessons or visualizing how to draft a pattern for a dress I was designing for myself or imagining the most efficient way of making a collar or a placket. Oh, there were always a million things that kept my mind busy, so many things I wanted to do. My problem was always finding enough time to do all the projects I wanted to do.

Jesus also said that I should have my hands chopped off if they should endanger my soul. Of course, I would not want to lose my hands, and I learned very young that I did not want to deal with guilt. When I was around six years old, I stole a nickel from Apang's pocket and the guilt that I felt made me feel so bad that I promised myself I would never want to feel guilty again. The same thing with telling lies. My life became more complicated when I told a lie. The first lie led to another lie to cover up the first lie and then to another until the network of lies became so complicated and my mind was in so much turmoil that I decided it was not worth it. By the time I got my little book, I was already a master of honesty; nothing is more beautiful than the truth.

People who knew me from way back, even my own siblings, in fact now that I think of it, including myself, never perceived me as an imitator of Christ. I never told anyone nor was I aware that I was imitating Christ. I was just following whatever was written in my little book, while at the same time, I was the active, bubbly young girl, very popular, a leader of all sorts of student activities, a member of the cheer leader team in high school, the best rock and roller, and awarded the honor of being the best folk dancer in my senior year in high school. I was so active in college too. When I graduated, the list of activities under my photograph must have been the longest in the whole Mapua Institute of Technology school of Architecture college yearbook of 1966. Although I was active in extracurricular activities, I was a mere conductor of meetings, I never expressed my opinions, majority rule was followed anyway.

Singing is another thing I love to do. I have been singing since I was a little girl. Every time it was my turn to do the dishes after dinner at home, I belted out all the songs I knew. Singing while washing dishes made me forget that I was doing a chore. I won a noontime amateur singing contest on television when I was sixteen, and I was with a quartet singing folk songs, aside from being a member of the college choir. The quartet I was a member of did mostly Peter Paul and Mary songs and I was doing Mary's part. We performed in several school functions and by popular demand, we held a concert at the MIT Philippines school campus to entertain the students.

Music is the language of the soul, so they say, and indeed it is a most soothing outlet for all my emotional turmoil. I sang my blues away during those moments when I felt so low. They say that it is healthy to vent grievances to someone and so I sang out my heart to my unseen pal Jesus who told me to cast my burdens unto him. Though invisible, he had always felt so real to me, and he did take my burdens away because after a heartfelt song offering him what tormented my heart or after praying fervently to him flat on my belly down on the floor in the privacy of my bedroom, asking him to help me carry my cross, he had always lifted up my soul, and I always felt better and my burden lighter when I got back up on my feet. I had sung to God in church services when I came to America sharing my feelings with the congregation. They must have liked listening to my songs of worship to my God because they invited me to share my songs with them many times.

Now that I look back on how this little book had influenced my life, I see all the benefits I acquired from it. The focus of my life was directed towards more personal growth-oriented matters. I was so curious about everything. I wanted to know the truth about everything. I used to enjoy reading novels, but soon, they did not satisfy me anymore. I became more interested in reading stories of events that really happened, the history of anything, the world, the different nations, human evolution physical and intellectual, science, I was searching for the absolute truth.

Aside from minding how to single-handedly bring up my children the best way I could, I became very thirsty for knowledge. All the informative programs on television became my entertainment. Through television, I relearned science and history in their most updated versions with the most beautiful graphic illustrations and scientific photographs. I operated on a very tight budget while raising my three children so I could not afford to travel, but television gave me the chance to see the world. I saw all the architectural wonders and the wondrous panoramic visions that different nations offered. I always had looked forward to the day when I would be able to afford real travel, and it did happen. I have set foot on all the seven continents of earth.

My interest in paleontology and anthropology confronted me with discrepancies between science and what I had learned from religion. This set me up to search for the absolute truth. I joined different Christian faiths. I was born Catholic, then I joined the Born-Again Christians, attended meetings of a group called Pentecostals, I became a Baptist and attended other Protestant churches, such as the Presbyterians and the

Methodist churches. Finally, I became a Seventh Day Adventist. Along the way, I also read handouts from Jehovah Witnesses, I attended Baha'i meetings, and watched Tv programs about Islam which didn't tell me much. I attended all sorts of Jewish festivities, asked my friends from India about their faith and I have read books by Ruth Montgomery about automatic writings. Christians believe that your soul go straight to heaven when you die, what then is reincarnation? I decided that for me to believe in reincarnation its confirmation must come from God. I was baptized with the name Pura Regalado when I was an infant in the Catholic faith and I was dunked in a water pool three other times submitting to the baptismal rituals of three other faiths. I wanted to know how one faith differed from another. I wanted to know what went on in the mind of every believer. I wanted to understand what motivated every individual to pursue life. I wanted to know what the truth is.

I realized that freedom from material want frees your mind to observe more closely and appreciate the things around you. You elevate your mind from mundane things to be one with nature to a point where you feel the exuberance and beauty of everything in the universe. I feel so much joy by merely looking at flowers, their simple elegance and fragrance or their beautiful colors and intricately designed petal arrangements never fail to catapult me into serene ecstasy. I feel wondrous energy bursting forth from the sprouting bud of a plant that is so full of life or the freshness of a new leaf on a tree making me greatly energized by their mere sight. I marvel at the beautiful landscapes, the beautiful foliage of the trees dancing with the wind, the soft delicate clouds that always try to impress me with their magnificent and glorious formations against the wondrous blue sky that at times turns softly purplish or radiant orange. The marvelous sunsets, all the heavenly gems in the sky at night, the crisp fresh mornings, every creature on earth, they all give me so much joy. Getting caught in traffic jams, no matter how long, even many hours at times caused by unfortunate accidents, never bothered me because nature kept me entertained until the traffic jams got untangled. Even thunderstorms at night are a great thrill to behold in the Florida evening skies where dancing lightning bolts stretch everywhere in violent outbursts covering almost the whole sky in a mysterious exciting rhythm that cannot be matched by any artificial fireworks. The sight of an innocent child at play brings back the happy memories of my children growing up. The helplessness of an infant always reminds me of the joyous moments when I sang my sweetest lullabies to put my babies to sleep. I see beauty in every being, in every creature. I feel the love of my children, brothers and sisters, and the loving memories of my mother and father, and the love of all other friends and relatives. I feel love in everything. Because down deep in my heart I know that I have done nothing wrong towards anybody, I enjoy a great inner peace that heightens the love I feel for every person on earth and everything in the universe. Being enraptured by these thoughts makes me experience Paradise but a Paradise that is still incomplete because of my sense of uselessness. If only I could find the true purpose of my life, then I could have truly claimed that I have found Paradise right here on earth.

Perhaps, I thought, if I can engage myself in some humanitarian activities, I am sure that would give purpose to my life, but I didn't know how to get started. I admire my youngest sister Elizabeth for what she has done. Right after finishing her studies to become a doctor, she devoted her young life to caring for the poor up in the boondocks, abandoning the comforts of city life to live with the poor in the remotest corner of my country of birth. The village she chose to serve was so remote that it could only be reached after a day long bus ride on a long-rugged dirt roads after which she had to walk for at least seven more miles along precariously narrow paths on the side of the mountains where one wrong step could mean falling down deep ravines. There were no other approaches, aside from wading across rivers with rushing waters that did not have bridges. It was a place with no electricity, no water supply, no plumbing, nor any kind of city comfort whatsoever. She learned to bathe in the cold rivers and live in the most primitive way after growing up in Manila with all the modern comforts of technology. She freely gave medical care to poor people who did not have any means of paying her back, save from sharing with her the meager produce of the mountains. I was so touched by the photographs she brought home every now and then when I was still back home in the Philippines. There was a picture of my dear sister in a bamboo raft with fresh provisions of sample medicine she had acquired from her trip to Manila while a couple of natives swam along beside the raft to guide it safely across the cold river to get her to her destination. The river, which was usually shallow enough to be crossed by wading on foot, had risen after a heavy rainfall. The people in the village appreciated what she was doing for them, so they all together put their efforts cutting down trees and bamboos to build her a clinic, a very primitive one, if you can imagine. I saw pictures of the natives busily putting the primitive structure together.

My sister Elizabeth's adventures in the remote mountains of the Philippines were full of dangers. During the Marcos regime, people like her were not understood, and what the regime did not understand, were assumed to be anti-government. A few others were doing the same work as she did, and they were all dispersed far away from each other helping the poor in their own ways, giving medical care to the people the government did not provide for. One of them got killed while on such a mission, shot by a Marcos soldier who suspected the poor young doctor of being a member of the NPA, an anti-government militant group called the National People's Army. These dangers did not deter my sister Elizabeth in her determination to carry out her self-imposed task.

I worked in an Architectural firm specializing in designs for the most luxurious homes. A big portion of our clientele consists of doctors who are so rich that they all want the most luxurious and spacious homes their money can buy. All the doctors whom I know wanted to become doctors because it is a fast way to become rich but not my sister Elizabeth. Many times, my mother had asked me to persuade my sister to stop what she was doing, to settle in Manila to start her own medical practice, just like her peers in medical college. I always answered, "Yes, Mom, I'll try," although deep in my heart, my thoughts were that, if I did not have my three little children to care for, I would have given her a hand in what she was doing.

I am sure there are many other humanitarians like Mother Teresa who are unheard of, my sister Elizabeth is one of them. What a coincidence that she too, like Mother Teresa, is a product of Loretto College where she got her primary and high school education before she went to the University of the Philippines for her degree in medicine. I am sure that Elizabeth's heart is full of joy because of what she accomplished because it is truly in giving that one finds true happiness, not in taking.

CHAPTER 3

I HAVE A DREAM

I daydream all the time about a project that I call Project HAPPY: H is for Help; A for Abrogate; P for Poverty; P for Please; Y for Yourself – Help Abrogate Poverty to Please Yourself. I find true joy in giving rather than in receiving. In fact, receiving gifts for me is more burdensome because it obligates me to reciprocate, whereas, when I give, to see that I made someone happy makes me happy enough and I don't expect any return for whatever I have given. Right now, the Mega Million jackpot is over a billion dollars. If I have that much money, I will create a solar panel farm which will be the housing for all the homeless with solar panel roofs and the occupants of these solar panel roofed homes will be the maintenance crew for the solar panel farms. These maintenance crew will be taught to grow or raise their own food so that the farm will be self-sufficient. Mother Teresa admirably devoted her life to taking care of the people who cannot take care of themselves anymore. My dream is to abrogate all causes of poverty. If no one would help me, I hope my book will sell and I will save all my royalties for this project. I hope and pray that my daydream of a farm where all poor people will learn to become self-sufficient, to be able to stand on their own feet without asking for alms to regain their lost dignity will come true.

What is so nice about daydreaming is that one has the freedom to fantasize about anything. Sometimes I fantasize about gradually buying all the tobacco farms on earth so as not to upset the world economy and converting them to a food farm or cotton farm, which would be more beneficial to mankind, If it were a cotton farm, then I would put up a textile mill also, to create more work for the people on my farm and I will provide them with housing with solar panel roofs. I am an Architect so I can design the housing facilities myself. The textile mills will produce fabrics that will sell for the same price as those outsourced to other countries with lower labor cost like China. Someone like my sister Elizabeth will be there to give everyone medical care and everyone will be educated to the highest level. There would be all sorts of facilities for cultural and sports activities and encouragement for everyone to develop their talents. I would want everyone to be happy and the only thing I would ask from these people on my farm is to create a crime-free community.

Energy produced by the solar panels will be sold to FPL in Florida and to other power distributors in the State or country where the solar Panel farms are. There will be fair profit sharing among all members of the crew working to operate the farm. I would save all my profits shares and buy more land and do it over and over until all the poverty on earth is abrogated. Wouldn't that be so nice? No more suffering anywhere. I must live a long life because I'm now retired and I only have my SS benefits to sustain me. If a mega rich philanthropist would donate a huge piece of land and help me start my Project HAPPY, the farm will be named after that generous donor!

We have heard of many mega rich people who cannot find their way to happiness, and they seek for escape from their misery through drugs and many had overdosed and died. It's because they cannot understand that it is in giving that they can find true happiness that they are searching for. Amassing more wealth is the only thing they desire which they believe is the way to the happiness they are searching for. Unfulfilled desire is among the major causes of unhappiness and depression.

Many will think that my dream is socialism, I have no problem with that because if my farm is in Florida, it will still be subject to Florida laws and the farm will abide with the laws. USA is a capitalist country, and it is motivated by greed, where the rich get richer, and the poor get poorer. I hope everyone will wake up to realize that greed is not the path towards true happiness. Corporations are outsourcing production of their merchandise not for the welfare of the consumers but for more profit for the investors. Corporations are continuously increasing prices of their commodities for more profit. Consumers on the other hand demand higher minimum wages. What good is raising minimum wages if the increase in their salaries will only be spent on the increase in prices of all commodities? It will only devaluate the dollar and the more USA cannot compete in the lower labor cost of other countries. If I can convince them to join me in my quest to abrogate poverty, that would bring them to their desired happiness.

This is the kind of fantasy that puts me to sleep every night or keeps my thoughts occupied when I am driving home on a dreary rainy day. I know that there is a means of eliminating poverty from the entire planet earth, and I also know that it will take time. Communism started from theories seeking for solutions to elimination of poverty but it did not work in the Soviet Union because people were not ready to accept such concepts and assured survival promised by Communism took away the challenge of competition to better themselves and many turned to alcoholism to escape the boredom that assured survival brought to their psyche.

In more than two decades that I had been a resident of USA, I have seen prices of commodities tripled, but the minimum wage barely doubled, meaning the buying power of the poor is getting less. There are more poor people than rich people. I don't understand why the majority does not rule. When would the poor majority realize that they should control rising prices of commodities imposed by the rich minority? If one entrepreneur raises prices of his goods, why do they encourage him by patronizing his products instead of abstaining from buying them to discourage raising of prices? What I see is that people seem to always need to improve their status quo, typical of a person with materialistic mentality who tries to get security from the amount of material things he can acquire, which is never enough. The more he gets, the more he wants. People seem to always need to prove to their peers that they too can afford to buy expensive things. I find it funny that celebrities who are paid mega bucks, wear designer outfits which I am sure were given to them free to entice consumers to buy these products, which are advertisements of the designers. The result is that everybody has become a walking billboard. If I were to advertise somebody's product, why should I pay for it? What is so beautiful about the designer's name painted or embroidered all over a shirt or a purse or a pair of shoes? What is the difference between that and a potato sack with the potato grower's name on it? Where is the aesthetic sense of humanity headed? Whenever I see a person wearing advertisement apparel, what I see is a person who is showing me the statement, "Look, I can afford this quality clothing too!" Is acquiring material things truly the key to happiness? I can mention of a lot of fabulously rich people who died of drug overdose because they tried to escape their miserable unhappiness on drugs.

It is written that it is easier for a camel to go through the eye of the needle than for a rich man to get to the kingdom of God. Didn't this insinuate that it is easier for the poor to get to the kingdom of God? Look at the conditions of impoverished communities; the crime rates are the highest. Shame on you poor people for letting God down. He was counting on you to show the rich that you can be happy in spite of your poverty. Instead, you allowed your communities to become Satan's playground. Now aside from being miserably poor, while you are still alive, you are going to be more miserable after you die, you will boil in the lake of fire until you become the dirt of the earth, dead forever, no more thinking, no more reasoning as a particle in lava, written in the Bible as – sinner soul cast to the lake of fire.

The law of supply and demand, which is the motivating force in a capitalistic society, is based on greed. What I see that results from this law of supply and demand is the continuing devaluation of the dollar and the growing number of impoverished people. Where will it end? This scenario reminds me of violent upheavals of the poor masses that almost every progressive nation went through, ending with the execution of the ruling class. There was King Charles I of England, King Louis XVI and Marie Antoinette of France, Nicholas and Alexandria of Russia. This happens over and over in the history of our world. That is why it is imperative that poverty be abrogated if we want to reach Utopia. When are we going to learn from our history? I hope Americans will do something now before matters go out of control. I am sure there is a peaceful means of eliminating poverty, which all the people of the world will agree to promulgate if we truly put our minds to finding it. Perhaps it would only happen when all of humanity finally comes to realize that true happiness comes not from greed but from generosity. I believe that this is the true reason why Christmas has a universal appeal. It is a season that triggers the generosity of men, which makes them truly happy. Only children enjoy receiving gifts. When you become a grown-up, giving becomes the true source of joy.

One evening, my children were watching a Star Trek episode on television, and my attention was caught by its depiction of a poverty free earth. I wanted to know how the writer of this episode purported to arrive at such an ideal situation. I started to watch the show regularly and before I knew it, I got completely hooked and I became a Trekkie. I have probably seen all the episodes, but I never saw one that explained how poverty was eradicated, and I was hoping that someone could give me other ideas how wealth could be dispersed more evenly all over the world. How can a single person like Bill Gates be worth a hundred Billion dollars when there are a billion people starving on earth? I wish I could find an answer. Anyway, I enjoyed the more optimistic view of the future of mankind unlike other science fiction stories that envision a very dreadfully bleak and gory future for planet earth. Some Star Trek episodes envisioning changes to our ways already happened. For instance, the show depicted a changed monetary system. I see cash money less and less and I don't even write checks anymore because my bills are automatically deducted from my bank account. All I carry is my bankcard, which all stores now honor. How nice it will be when bio-scans become a reality where all is needed is the imprint of my hand on a bio-scanner for identification, no more bank card is needed. I hope they discover a scanner with non-carcinogenic rays.

Meanwhile, back to my search for a purpose. There was an incident that made me toy with the idea that perhaps I would be very useful to humanity if in my own way I could prove that when Jesus said – He who believes in me shall not die, - he truly means not to die physically. The science channel repeatedly try to prove that the shroud of Jesus on display in Torino, Italy is fake. Ignoring the fact that this shroud had gone through a fire where the heat could have cooked and changed its molecular structure making accurate carbon dating no longer viable, aside from a painting depicting this shroud done years before the date derived from carbon dating, proving the inaccuracy of the carbon dating. The last one I saw was the science channel showing the blood flow across the back waist of Jesus, which they say was impossible to happen. What I saw is that the science channel presented proof that Jesus was alive when he raptured body and soul to be one with God in eternal life. He turned to his side, thus, the blood flowing from his chest wound from a spear, flowed across his back waist when he turned to his side, therefore, he was alive!

Jesus said – Come follow me. It is also written in John 3:16 that Whosoever believeth in him should not perish but have everlasting life. Revelation 21:4 says: Death shall be no more – because when we rapture body and soul to be one with God, we no longer leave lifeless cadavers as what Jesus accomplished, and he said – Come and follow me. I am taking these words literally. I am trying to stay alive until I metamorphose body and soul to be one with God in eternal life. If I fail, then I am sure I shall be born again or reincarnate. John 3;13 says – no one has ascended to heaven except he who came down from heaven. The Christian belief that you go straight to heaven when you die is false. God is the God of the living and not of the dead. No dead enters heaven. Jesus said – you need to be born again – confirming the Buddhist belief in reincarnation. Protestants preach that you do not need to be perfect because the blood of Jesus saved you already, which is blasphemy! Jesus said – You need to be perfect to reach the kingdom of heaven.

I had this nagging whisper in my ear that the true message of the story of Adam and Eve was obscured by the myth of creation which the science of paleontology debunked. Adam and Eve were supposed to be immortals if they did not sin, but they started to face death after falling into sin. Therefore, if the voice in the wind whispering in my ear that if we don't sin, we will be immortals, is true, overcoming death has become a major challenge in my life. When I joined the Seventh Day Adventists, I found out that they are the only belief system that correctly follow the commandment Keep thou holy the Sabbath day. They interpret this commandment as referring to physical health. Indeed, if we are aspiring for immortality, we must keep our body in good health. Seventh Day Adventists forbids drinking alcohol and eating pork. I never drank any alcoholic beverages when I was still in the Philippines but with my new husband, I learned to drink beer once a week and 4 Oz, sangria wine every night. Anyway, Jesus said that it is not what you put in your mouth but what comes out of your mouth that defiles you.

To overcome death, I have to make my plan of action. I must do everything that will keep me healthy. That drove me to keep an eye on everything that discussed longevity. I combed every issue of every periodical that came my way long before longevity magazines came into publication. One researcher observed that the hypothalamus glands of an infant is plump like a juicy ripe berry while that of an aged man or woman is shriveled and small like a raisin. He theorized that the brain produces harmful chemicals every time every time a person experiences anxiety or stress. He said that when the Hypothalamus gland, which is also responsible for the immune system, is under attack, the immune system becomes weak, and the person becomes susceptible to illnesses. Therefore, I should avoid any stress or any negative emotions that will endanger my hypothalamus gland, I must protect this precious gland diligently to win my war.

I have an advantage, I thought. I already have a weapon against negative emotions; my precious little book had already taught me how to deal with disappointments since I was sixteen. The seven deadly sins also came to my mind. I then realized how profound it is that they are called deadly. They indeed kill the body literally when one fails to overcome the bad feelings these negative emotions evoke because the body produces the death agents or free radicals that ravages all the organs and cause them to age and malfunction. I must therefore avoid anger, envy, pride, avarice, greed, gluttony and sloth, and all other negative emotions and I must stay cool, no matter what. I don't have any problem with lust, greed and sloth because I am not lustful, greedy or lazy, but I realized that other people who are lustful, greedy and slothful can cause you to produce free radicals in your body because of the frustrations they cause you. Bert was so lustful, and he had caused me severe heartache, and Nick was so greedy that I could not take him back when he asked me to. I encountered another man Ville, who was the epitome of slothfulness whenever he was with me. It seemed that my capabilities evoked slothfulness in him. I had no choice but to stay away from him. On his own, without me, he seemed to be alright.

Every time I encounter a person behaving obnoxiously, I remind myself - Oh no! You're not making me produce free radicals! No no no no no! You can keep the free radicals for yourself but don't contaminate me! I have to fiercely protect my hypothalamus glands if I want to win this war against death! There were times when extreme cases came along when I could not avoid getting irritated. So, I know I still have to work on mastering the art of eluding all these negative emotions.

Longevity researchers also said that our body was designed to live forever, but we are doing something wrong, which is why we age and eventually die. They say that aging is a disease. Could it be that what makes us old is committing sin? Is our body programmed to self-destruct every time we sin? I would describe sin as anything disruptive of the harmony of nature and anything that hurts people, including yourself. When we sin, we hurt someone, so harmony is disrupted. Therefore, if I don't sin, then I should not die. The only way I can prove this theory is to conduct an experiment, just like an experiment in a physics lab. I will not sin from here on and see where this experiment will take me. I hope God will forgive me for whatever sins I have committed in the past. This will also put to test the power of autosuggestion, All we see happening to man is that one is born, then grows old, then dies. We accept the fatalistic notion that life always ends in death. We submit ourselves to this fate. We expect that we too will die like everyone else, therefore we will ourselves to die, and our body follows what is in our minds. It looks to me that Jesus tried to change this outlook two thousand years ago, but no one took him seriously. Well, I'm ready to take his words completely literally. I have been following the words of Jesus all my life. I might as well follow everything he says to the end no matter how impossible it sounds. If he said it, it should happen and let the future show me where this kind of mentality will lead me.

The beings of angels also came to my mind. What really is an angel? Angels had been mentioned many times in the Bible, but we do not know where they are from or how they came into being. Could an angel be a being who has reached perfection in body, mind and soul and metamorphosed into omnipotence? Is that how we humans can reach the highest level of existence that we call heaven? Is our human form the caterpillar that would metamorphose into a beautiful butterfly that is the angel? It dawned on me that the body of Jesus disappeared after his crucifixion. Every atom of his body must have converted into spirit, a state of pure energy. Did Jesus come to show us what the human body would become if we were perfect like him?

While watching Star Trek episodes, I found ideals parallel to my quest for everlasting life. There was one episode where the Star Trek crew found a humanoid from another planet severely injured in a spacecraft crash. The doctor could not do anything to save him and yet this highly evolved being's body regenerated itself back to health on its own, and in the end metamorphosed into an entity of pure spirit. It came to my mind that the fantasy of the writer of that episode was parallel to my own thinking. Did he also tap into a higher source of knowledge? I am not alone!

The Star Trek character "Q" is an omnipotent being. Although Q was mischievous, his mischief had limits. When he went beyond this limit. He turned back into a mortal vulnerable to physical death. I found it exciting to toy with the idea that being like Q would be the ultimate result of my quest for an unending life. Wouldn't it be grand if I could explore all the quadrants in the universe and explore all the different life forms on other planets if I were omnipotent like Q? My quest to prove John 3:16 became more exciting.

An Astronaut stayed in the space station for a year and came back down to earth with muscles completely atrophied. He had to be carried from the spacecraft to a wheelchair. Even human eyes get adversely affected by weightlessness. It appears that we humans have not physically evolved to tackle long space travels. How can an alien from another solar system hundreds of lightyears away avoid the deleterious effect of weightlessness? Before I can believe that an alien from a planet like earth can come to our planet, I would like answers to my questions first. Otherwise, I say that all phenomena about alien sightings and visitations and alien abduction stories are manifestations of archetypes that emanated from our collective unconscious created by collective beliefs and fears of aliens.

A lot of researchers are bent on finding out what it is we are doing wrong that makes us old. They say aging is a disease. They say that if are doing everything right, we should stay young. Some are even looking at genetic engineering, aiming to produce a genetically perfect human. Granted that they are able to produce this genetically perfect human being, would this being be able to prevent the production of free radicals if confronted with negative emotions? I believe that even a genetically perfect being would still need to master the art of avoiding all negative emotions to triumph over death.

The cost of man-made devices for staying young is well beyond my financial capability. I have no other choice than to rely on what Jesus said, man does not live on bread alone but by all the words that come from God, and he also said that it is harder for a rich man to enter the kingdom of God. God would not say that if immortality can only be reached by spending a fortune. The joy I feel and the energy I get from being one with nature is my natural antioxidant and each time I feel the exuberance that nature arouses in me, I tell myself, feel the love of God and be energized and rejuvenated, get younger and younger and let the future unfold.

Nutrition and proper body care are also important if I want to have life forever. Researchers say that almost all diseases are caused by malnutrition. I am very fortunate that I was bunched up with people who gradually turned into health freaks right before my eyes, At work, our company President is a perfect picture of ageless youth, and so is our vice president Maria, who is so fanatical about staying young. She tirelessly clipped all articles with prescriptions that will contribute to the body's wellbeing and passes it around for everyone to read. Dan, an office mate who is my platonic sidekick, takes hundreds of health supplement pills every day. Eating the right food was always everybody's concern. As for me, I eat whatever my taste buds crave for, and I was glad to find out that the articles that Maria clipped about nutrition proved to me that my taste buds has been guiding me to eat the right food all along. All the whole crew members of the company goad each other to stay physically fit. All of us were aiming for long life. I worked with this company for 15 years and I saw them awaken to the pursuit of longevity. They did not know that I on my own way, years before, had already been challenging to prove that John 3:16 means literally. Although we were all in pursuit for long life, my quest goes beyond longevity. Mine is to reach immortality. In our common pursuit, our methods were different because I cannot afford their means of reaching our common goal. All of them are taking all sorts of pills, antioxidants, supplements, et cetera, while I rely only on natural food and the words of God. I am not taking any kind of pill whatsoever, including contraceptives. My body always reacts adversely to all these pills. The end will show the more effective method, and the contest is a foot.

When the Bible was written, the messenger who said to Eve that he who eats the fruit of knowledge shall be like God was vilified and it was portrayed as a lowly venomous snake. The message of Jesus is basically – science is the absolute truth: Eve is a woman who picked the fruit of knowledge and gave it to Adam. False beliefs will prevent one from achieving purity of mind required to reach perfection. I am a woman whom God bestowed upon these truths that I am sharing with humanity.

Meanwhile while I was pursuing physical immortality, which all Christians will think idiotic, I thought that if I found a partner, whom I could love and care for and whom I could make happy, that would be a good purpose for my life while I am unable to get my project HAPPY in operation. Unfortunately, finding the right partner for me had been most difficult. I could not find the man suitable for me. In the first month of 1994, I dated a Dean of a University. I was so excited to meet someone with a doctorate in engineering degree. I looked forward to an exciting intellectual conversation with him. After watching La Boheme at a theater down in Miami, we had dinner in a nice cozy restaurant. At first, we talked about the places he had traveled to. Then our conversation wandered to history, and he started to mention that the first man to circumnavigate the world was a Portuguese whose name he could not remember. I quickly replied, "He was Fernando Magallanes, Magellan in English, he was Portuguese but his expedition across the Pacific was under the flagship of Spain." I became so enthusiastic about the subject he started because it led to the European discovery of what became the land of my birth in the far east. I was so eager to narrate everything I knew, and it became apparent that he was not so well versed about it. I saw a hint of embarrassment on his face. So I tried to change the topic of our conversation back to Spain, which he had recently visited. I asked him about the Escorial. I had always been interested in Spain, which for some reason, I had felt a link with. Perhaps it was because the culture of my people had been greatly influenced by this once upon a time powerful country that colonized the Philippines for three hundred seventy-five years. It was awesome to think that the remains of King Charles V, who was the king of Spain when Magellan sailed across the Pacific to my homeland, and his son Philip II, the king in whose honor my country was named after, were in El Escorial.

The thought of a mausoleum suddenly reminded me of a show on television and I started sharing it with my date. It was about the bones of men, particularly that of a boy of around twelve years of age unearthed in a cave called Kafsi in Israel. This TV program named the bones of the boy, the Kafsi cave boy. What was so fascinating about this Kafsi cave boy was that he could be the skeleton of any twelve-year-old boy of today and yet biochemists had dated his remains to be between ninety thousand to one hundred thousand years old. I started telling my date that the Cro-Magnon man's remains were dated to be only forty-five thousand years old, very much younger than the Kafsi boy, but was still very primitive with huge powerful jaws. In his attempt to add to the conversation, he said, "The dinosaurs were still on earth at that time." Without thinking, I immediately but softly corrected him, "Oh no, the dinosaurs went extinct about sixty-six million years ago." This time, he could not hide the embarrassment on his countenance anymore.

After that disastrous evening, he never asked me out again. I started to ask myself if I should play dumb to catch a man, but no, that would be dishonest, and I could not be dishonest. Why would anyone be embarrassed to admit that he does not know every subject matter on earth, which is but normal? I would not pretend that I know everything. It just so happened that at that particular moment the subject of paleontology crept into my mind and I wanted to share with him my enthusiasm about it. Anyway, I believe it is for the best to find out if you can talk to a person or not while on the early dating stage before getting into any emotional involvement, I don't think it would be fun to be with someone for whom you have to tread on thin ice in order to please. The Kafsi cave boy, I thought, deserved some attention. His hundred-thousand-year-old bones could be evidence of the possibility of someone going through a time warp to the past and getting trapped there. That would be like the Star Trek episode where Data's head was found in a cave and had been dated to be in that cave for five hundred years before he and the rest of the Star Trek crew went through the time warp. Wouldn't it be amazing if someone uncovered a record of a family in our present era that had disappeared mysteriously without any trace and whose characteristics or DNA would match those bones in Kafsi? Whooow, I could hear the melody of the Twilight Zone theme music humming in my ears. That would really be spooky. Who knows, perhaps UFOs are our descendants on our own planet Earth who have developed the technology to travel back in time, and back to the future. If that is the case, then we should not be afraid of these UFOs.

Another man who caught my attention was Mr. GI Joe, a Vietnam War veteran and a retired policeman. Joe was not in any way near my intellectual level, but he was not at all bothered by it and his boyishness appealed to my motherly instinct. When I got to know him better, I realized how the Vietnam War had left him scarred for life. At the time I met Joe, I had a marriage proposal from Dennis, a contract worker at Ames Design. I knew that there were a lot of other women who would be very happy to be the wife of Dennis. Joe who could not hold on to a relationship with a woman because of the emotional turmoil resulting from his VW experience, needed me more. He aroused my compassion. I could imagine how terrible it must have been for the very young men who were sent to that terrible war. I thought that it would give my life more meaning if I could make this Vietnam War veteran happy even if the only kind of relationship, he was capable of was platonic in nature. With a platonic relationship, I would not have to deal with the guilt of fornication, I thought.

Joe was still an active member of the armed forces, and he still went to annual military training. One time he asked me to help him redecorate his home while he was away on training. He chose teal color for the carpet and the Italian ceramic tile that he liked and left everything else to me. I was happy to oblige. I very much enjoy home decorating, especially when I was not the one responsible for the major expenses. I stayed in his home supervising the workers while he was away. For finishing touches, I bought two canvases and a few tubes of oil paints, and I painted a replica of a Georgia O'Keeffe museum piece on one of the canvases and I reproduced Cezanne's Man with a Pipe to hang on the empty walls in the living room. I had not done any oil painting for at least a decade, and I did not want to take chances on doing originals. I just wanted to produce something that suited my taste as fast as I could at the least expense before Joe arrived. I did not copy the face of the man with a pipe Cezanne's original, Instead, I painted Joe's face of how he looked like when he got out of Vietnam. I made two velvet throw pillows, one purple and one teal, to accentuate the brand-new white leather couch and love seat, which Joe purchased. A bedroom ensemble of teal overall print on white background looked perfect in his bedroom. For his bathrooms I bought flush towel sets also in teal color with a touch of purple to carry out the color scheme. For finishing touches, I propped live plants everywhere. I just love decorating with live indoor plants that absorb carbon dioxide and emits oxygen indoor. I was quite happy with the overall effect of the project.

Gardening was something I had always wanted to do but never had the chance to do it. Joe's home had a yard that needed attention. I was very happy when Joe gave me a free hand on what to do with it. It was the very first time in my life that I tried gardening. I learned to ride the shovel so my body weight would drive it down into the dirt to loosen the soil, like a little girl having the fun of her life. I never knew how complex the crisscrossing network of grass roots was until I tried to clear the plot where to plant my flower seedlings.

At work, one of our clients was a United Airline pilot named John who did his own gardening. He came to our office for the design of a hangar for his own personal plane next to his huge house and the job was assigned to me. He had invited me twice to his home and I was ecstatic when I saw his tropical garden, which he tended to himself. He did not hire a gardener to do it for him. I was so envious of his wonderfully gorgeous garden and how I wished to have the chance to try my own gardening too. This sweet intelligent pilot, a brother of a Florida councilor, was obviously very wealthy to have a real airplane for a toy. Yet I saw him without any hesitation, dig down in the dirt with his bare hands to fix a plant. While I was his guest, we went to Home Depot to buy the fittings for more lines for his sprinkler system, and I was so impressed that he even knew how to do the sprinkler system himself. I was in awe to see this millionaire who when not piloting a UA plane was a gardener in his own yard. I came to understand John perfectly when I was given the chance to do gardening at Joe's yard.

Watching a seed from almost nothing to something, then a seedling growing and blossoming into a beautiful plant was a thrill that made me feel how it was to be God.

While I was in the middle of my interior decorating stint, I got a call from a man named Robert. He said that Rabbi Sherman gave him Joe's number and introduced himself as the father of Richard, another Vietnam War veteran just like Joe. He was looking for someone who could be Richard's friend and since Joe was a more fortunate VW veteran who did not suffer physical injuries like his son, who might be willing to add a little color to Richard's life by being his friend. Richard was confined in a home for disabled people only a couple of miles from Joe's place. I was touched by Robert's concern for his son's happiness, and I volunteered to visit Richard while Joe was still away. Richard was a tall man whose features showed every indication that he was a handsome young man when the government sent him to that awful war. I did not see immediately how he was injured until he spoke. I then realized that his injury impaired his ability to speak clearly. He was unable to control the flow of air from his lungs to produce distinct consonant sounds, which made it difficult for me to understand him at first. I saw a chess set on the wall shelf and I remembered Robert telling me that he was a good chess player. I asked him if he would play chess with me, and he eagerly agreed. Whenever I fully concentrate on my game, I usually beat a male opponent whose ability is on the same level as mine because they tend to be overconfident playing with a woman. Seeing Richard completely focused on his game, making very careful well thought out moves took my thoughts away from the chessboard, I could not stop thinking that if he could play chess, then his brain must still be functioning normally, perhaps normal enough to operate a computer. I kept wondering if other avenues that could possibly give more meaning to his existence had been investigated instead of him being cooped up in that home with other invalid people because I could see him move around like any normal person. Richard won our chess match, and I was glad that I was able in a way to add a little fun to his life.

When Joe came back from his two weeks military training, I told him about Richard only to find out that he did not want to have anything to do with anyone who reminded him of his nightmarish existence in Vietnam. I fully understood Joe but I continued to visit Richard because I started a friendship with him, which I could not terminate just like that. On my subsequent visits, Richard's speech became a little more comprehensible to me and we managed to communicate better although I still saw many occasions when he got very frustrated when I could not understand what he was trying to tell me. One time he held my hand and gave me a grand tour of the yard and introduced me to all their pets. A dog, a bunny rabbit, a goat, a goose, and also a pig. Another time he asked me for a ride, and I agreed. I did not have the heart to refuse him. After getting permission from the care takers, off we went around the vicinity. We found an eatery along the way and had a snack, I usually did not carry cash with me but I was glad I had enough for both of us on that unexpected gallivanting spree. Joe was only a couple of miles away and I thought of introducing Richard to him, so we stopped by. I thought that if Joe saw how normal Richard was, except for his speech, he might change his mind and agree to be Richard's friend. I thought they might be able to confront and discard each other's demon from that war if they could be friends. My unexpected visit to Joe became a fiasco. He was entertaining a lady friend whom he did not want me to know about.

It turned out that Joe was a chronic liar who took me on an endless emotional roller coaster. It was I whom he had taken to all his Jewish family gatherings and to all his retired police friends' get-togethers, yet he satisfied his sexual urges with this woman. His explanation was that I was a decent woman, and he could not do those kinds of things with me. I did not mind being just a friend to him if he would only be honest with me. He begged me not to leave him for another man, promising to go for therapy to solve his emotional problems. I ended my relationship with him countless times, but he knew how to play with my soft heart, so I ended up giving him another chance.

A week after I met Joe, he introduced me to his friend Kathleen. It was Kathleen who finally came to my rescue from Joe's cunning devices. She convinced me that Joe will never change. She became my very good friend and confidant. I realized that meeting Joe was just the road that led me to meeting Kathleen. I never had a close lady friend whom I opened my heart to the way I did to her. With her influence, I started looking after myself, the self that was nonexistent before I met her. Whenever I get into a relationship with a man, I never asked what that man can do for me, all that mattered to me was what I could do for him. This attitude, she told me, indicated that I did not love myself and that I could not give love if I did not love myself. She said, "You cannot give what you do not have."

Kathleen's remarks sent me into deep thoughts. My little book taught me to love everyone and everything, but did it teach me to love myself? I started to wonder. Imitating Christ taught me to be nonexistent. How could I love myself if I did not exist? "Let there be not me but you shining through me" was one of the prayers I borrowed from one of his devoted followers. Where was the love I felt for everyone, for everything around me coming from? Wasn't that feeling from me? I thought I was overflowing with love for everyone until Kathleen put it in a human perspective.

Joe's repeated cunning lies was hurting me badly and producing free radicals inside me, so with Kathleen's encouragement to start thinking for myself, I decided that I could no longer let Joe hurt me further. I avoided him and asked our secretary not to let his numerous calls go through to me anymore. I got myself a caller ID at home so I would know when not to pick up the phone when it rang. Although I stopped seeing Joe, I continued to visit Richard, but I started to sense something that made me feel a bit uncomfortable, especially when he asked me if I was married, and he kissed me on my cheek when I said goodbye on one of my visits. I did not want to hurt him, but I was afraid he was getting the wrong signal about my true motive for seeing him. I let a couple of months pass before I visited him again and when I did, he told me not to see him anymore. I felt a little hurt in my heart, but it was good that it came from him and not from me. It was for the best. That was the end of my episode with two Vietnam War veterans.

There was another sweet John who became a very good friend of mine. Just like John the Pilot, he was also a very nice bachelor. John was in the same Bible class that I attended while I was a member of the Seven Day Adventist Church. He was an insurance agent when I met him and later on, he became a physical therapist. I enjoyed the clean wholesome friendships I had with these two Johns. John the pilot's home was in a development with a landing strip lined on each side with two rows of beautiful soft tiny blue lights that came daintily aglow at night accentuated by pretty little red lights at the ends. I remember our running down the landing strip hand in hand, just like little children enjoying the moment. My white eyelet dress flowed with the wind and my white platform shoes got muddy as we ran. John had a detached guesthouse where I stayed overnight on both occasions when I was his guest. It was so refreshing to be assured that real gentlemen still exist in our adulterous generation and that not all guys are like what heroes in movies are portrayed who get lovey dovey with all women who cross their paths.

Being with John the PT was a duplication of being with John the Pilot. Hours went by unnoticed every time we chatted on the phone about all sorts of things that came to our minds. Whether we were watching a jazz concert, or the fireworks on July fourth at the park, or joining church activities such as feeding the homeless or entertaining the aged, his company had always been a delight for me. I regret that I could not carry on this kind of relationship with him when he finally got married, but we both did not want to create complications in his new marriage. I felt sorry for him when he shared with me a letter he got from one of the members of the Seventh Day Adventist Church telling him that he had allowed Satan to rule over him when he married a woman of the Baptist faith. How can anyone make such a judgement? I was very disappointed. SDA members pride themselves as being the most well versed of the Bible and yet they overlooked what Jesus said, Judge not so ye not be judged. What makes one church believe that its faith is better than another especially when both worship Jesus as God? These differences in belief systems are the seas that separate people from each other. It was time to continue my search for the truth. I ended my membership with the SDA thereafter.

CHAPTER 4

While I was so absorbed in my role as a mother, I did not have time to develop a deep friendship with anyone. Those whom I knew were mere acquaintances that I invited over for dinner. That was my only form of social life. The few gentlemen I already mentioned were casual friends. There was another gentleman named Jeff and my workmate and platonic sidekick Dan and another lady named Midge. They were the only ones who became close friends, but I never learned to cry on their shoulders. I did not want to burden anyone with my troubles, not even my own sister Anita. My world was confined around my children and my activities were around home, work, church, my children's school, and shops where we get our necessities. Whatever my children did I did too. When they were teenagers, I was doing everything teenagers did too. My children shared with me whatever caught their attention, whether it be a magazine or a movie, or a television show or a game or just anything. I heard of grown-ups not enjoying movies geared for teenagers, but not me. When I saw Wayne's World with my children, I was giggling throughout the show with them. I must have been the oldest viewer at the movie house when I went with the kids to see the Rocky Horror movie flick, where the kids went armed with water pistols and other paraphernalia to join in the action. When I went to Bush Gardens and the Water Park, I was with them on every ride, even riding the Kumba twice.

I never really had the chance to be aware of the outlook of other people regarding life until I met Kathleen who was very supportive of me while I was in the process of healing from the emotional pain that Joe had caused me. She encouraged me to open up. She was one person who made me feel that she was willing to carry the load on my shoulder with me. Before I met Kathleen, Jesus was my only friend whom I confided in and believe it or not Jesus was very real to me. I felt his warm comforting presence especially when I went to bed alone at night. Every time things became too heavy for me to bear; I fervently implored him for help. In the privacy of my bedroom, I humbled myself down on the floor flat on my belly with my hands stretched out, making the figure of the cross with my body. He never failed me. Every time I humbled myself before him, I got up feeling lighter, no longer pressured by the weight of my problem. Because of my relationship with Jesus, I did not have any need for a close friend. When I met Kathleen, I discovered that I could share my emotional load with a human too, and it was very comforting.

After meeting with Kathleen, I decided to have sessions with a psychotherapist. In the past, I always thought that I would never need the help of a psychoanalyst, who to me were just humans who have problems of their own. I could not convince myself that they would be able to help me. I thought that my religion was all I needed until I met Kathleen. Her outlook aroused my curiosity.

My therapist was a client at Ames Design where I worked. Our company designed a beautiful Japanese style home for her and her husband. She was a very considerate woman who understood my financial situation and gave me the sessions that I needed for a fifth of her normal rate. It was so kind and generous of her. For ten months, I went to meet with her at seven in the morning every week. She was such a delightful therapist that I looked forward to each session with her. Her name was Kathleen Ruskin. While I was having therapy with Kathleen R., Kathleen was my emotional anchor. What a happy coincidence that they were both named Kathleen, which is a derivative of Catherine. A fellow member of the choir I had joined recently, told me that in Gaelic, Cathy, a nickname for Catherine, means pure, just like my name. I had a dream that I was Queen Catherine of Aragon.

Kathleen and Kathleen R. taught me to be human. Because of them, I started to think that I would not find a full human life because I was trying to be a god. I was following everything in my little book, The Imitation of Christ. I was imitating Christ. As a Christian, I was indoctrinated that Christ is the appearance of God in human form, therefore He is a God, but I am just a mere mortal human.

The two Kathleens showed me why my relationships with a man never worked. Since I never asked myself what a man could do for me whenever I accepted a man for a partner, I never considered what kind of a person I was accepting in my life. I had been so blind to all the shortcomings of the men I accepted in my life because I was not looking for any. Since I have this deep feeling of love for all mankind, anyone who wanted to be my partner was welcome whenever I was not committed to anyone, an attitude that led me to failed horrible marriages. If I had met a man who was also trying to be a god, perhaps it would have worked, but where on earth can one find such a man? I promised myself that If ever I would accept another man in my life, he would have to be someone ideally suited for me or none at all. It is a human need to have a partner. Jesus was not human; he did not need a partner. While I still need a human partner, I couldn't fully imitate Christ. If I wanted to completely be like Jesus, I would have to learn to be alone without a partner.

My outlook made a complete turnaround. I started developing a social life with real friends. My focus went to sport activities, which were so much fun. I started playing tennis with Kathleen and her tennis buddies, Jim and Jennifer. Jim is an avid skier and through Jim and Kathleen, I started learning to ski. Jim and Kathleen advised me to learn to roller blade because, according to them, I would learn to ski faster if I knew how to balance myself with roller blades. I started playing tennis, rollerblading and skiing at the age of half a century and what a great time I had! I was a child again, just having fun playing!

While my whole life had started to become fun for me, Kathleen started having depression of her own. She had been so generous to me with her time when I needed her. I wanted to return her kindness. She was looking for a roommate so I told her that I would rent one of her rooms. I told her that I would be closer to my work if I rented one of her rooms. Her home was not really that much closer, it was around seventeen miles against my twenty-five miles drive from my condominium apartment to work. I wasn't giving up my condo apartment, I expected that all my children would come back home after college. The eight miles daily savings on gas expense wasn't really worth a room's rent, but what is money between friends? She had been there for me when I was down, I wanted to keep her company until she overcame her own depression.

At Kathleen's home, a little corner with votive candles and a sort of an altar aroused my curiosity. Kathleen explained to me that she meditated in that corner, and she told me about a mantra that she chants while meditating to raise her consciousness to a higher level. I thought of monks I saw on television humming while in deep thoughts, and I started imagining Kathleen doing the same thing. I found it interesting that a woman of Jewish origin was practicing a Buddhist ritual. If that was the way she could raise her consciousness to a higher level, good for her! I thought being aware of everything that goes on in our world, filling your mind with all the knowledge the whole world offers, elevating your thoughts from the mundane and being aware of the beauty of the whole universe, is what would raise your consciousness to a higher level, I wondered how one's consciousness would be raised if you keep you mind empty. Do people who meditate with empty minds expect a divine power to lift their consciousness and fill their minds with knowledge? She borrowed a book from the public library entitled "Ageless Body, Timeless Mind" by Deepak Chopra. She kept saying that it was a great book while reading it, but her enthusiasm did not arouse my interest because I had read a book of the Maharishi way back in the seventies. What more would this Deepak say that I don't know yet? I thought.

On Mother's Day of 1998, I came upon some tapes of Deepak Chopra's lectures, and by that time, my curiosity had already been aroused to find out what he was talking about, After watching his tapes, I went to the library and borrowed the same book Kathleen was reading, the Ageless Body, Timeless Mind, It was amazing. He was lecturing about the same thing that I had set up my mind to pursue. He even mentioned that we are probably gods in embryo. It was very encouraging to see that although we had taken different paths, our pursued destination is the same. His path must have started with Hinduism or Buddhism and mine from Christianity.

Spending more time with Kathleen made me realize that our worlds were not completely the same. She had a big throng of lady friends. One time they organized a ladies only birthday party for her. They decided to go to a strip joint where the strippers were men. I had never been to any of these kinds of places, but they all convince me to come along. I did not want to go with them, but while I was driving on my way home, I saw all of them in a big van waving at me, telling me to follow. I decided that their extraordinary gesture of wanting me to be with them deserved to be reciprocated, so I agreed. I followed them down to Miami. I was glad that I went to that tumultuous place driving my own car because five minutes later, I was back in my car to find my way home again.

That was my very first voyage to have a glimpse of a different world. Lo and behold, magnificent human species practically naked except for a miniscule pouch held in place with strings to cover their genitalia. They were all parading their beautifully built bodies, some gyrating erotically, some jumping up and down the dice, some climbing up the framework above while some women came close to them to slip paper bills into their pouch to be rewarded by a kiss or a peek into the secret hidden by the pouch. Women were drinking and smoking and cheering the show in a manner that made me not want to look. Everything in that place was so repulsive to me. They were all humans acting like monkeys. A chimpanzee dressed as a human is adorable and funny, but I found humans acting like monkeys pathetic. Perhaps they thought I was pathetic too, to feel the way I did, but that was a matter of opinion. If one believes happiness can be found by acting like an animal, well, so be it. My little book told me not to judge so that no one would judge me. I cannot imagine how that utter turbulent earthly world can make one experience the serene joy and happiness that I have found in my world. This reminded me of the three mythical monkeys: see no evil, says one of them. I have seen but could I judge if what I had seen was evil? Did I sin because I saw? I don't think so. In fact, I have learned how diverse life can be.

I had learned more about life by associating with Kathleen. I had learned not to depend on anyone for my happiness. When I stopped depending on others to give meaning to my life, when I became once again a child, I finally reached paradise right here on earth. Jesus said that one has to be converted and be like a child to enter the Kingdom of God, which must be what it means. I felt so happy being like a child again, gliding down the slopes in my skis. I felt I was in heaven gliding down the slopes in Steamboat Springs called: Why Not" snow plowing all the way just like the little kids alongside me, from the top of the mountain down to the bottom. It was my very first-time skiing. Thank God I have powerful thighs that could snow plow the whole length of the slope. Yes, oh yes! I was a child again but this time, a child with wisdom! I felt like Adam in Paradise, an Adam that is a woman, shouting with joy, "God, I'm here in Paradise, talk to me! You said that if I reach Paradise, you will talk to me. I'm here now! My ears are wide open to listen to you!"

I also talk to plants all the time. I know that there are people who think that doing this is being a kook, but they are the ones missing a bunch. When you are in Paradise, the plants and trees and flowers, the clouds, all the celestial bodies, the animals and everything on earth talk back to you when you talk to them. Every time I admiringly behold these wonderful creatures and creations, they all tell me, "Look at me, see how beautiful I am. I'm here to make your world breathtakingly exciting and colorful. I am here to entertain you and energize you and make you happy!" Because of this, everyday I am so full of energy for facing the exciting challenges of work at the office. I finally found life and how truly wonderful it is. Not only that, now I know what love really means. The kind of love Kathleen knows is different from what I know. I don't love for me. I don't need to love myself to give love to another. Some people mistake strong physical attraction for love when it is nothing but lust. Some people mistake a great craving for someone or something as love when it is nothing but greed or selfish desire which causes pain when the desire is unfulfilled. The love I know is unconditional, it does not need anything in return. I love because of love.

Buddha was right: sorrow is the result of unfulfilled desire. I stopped desiring for a purpose for my life and I never had any desire for anything material for myself in the first place, so now there was really nothing more that can give me sorrow. Even people who get nasty arouse my compassion instead of annoyance because I now understand that their nastiness is the result of their desire for everything to go their way all the time. Jesus taught me to put myself last. I give priority to the needs of others before mine. Although Buddha was right in what he preached, it was Jesus who showed me the path to Paradise. Those people who became Monks to escape the world, I wonder if they feel the same happiness I feel. What about the three mythical monkeys who say: see no evil; hear no evil; speak no evil? The only way you can follow the advice of these mythical monkeys is to hide in a monastery, just as Monks do. Out in the world, there is no way you can avoid seeing and hearing evil, but Jesus has a formula for not letting what you see or hear to corrupt you. I found happiness not by running away from the world but by facing it head on. I know someday I will be useful to humanity, but for the moment, I decided to enjoy Paradise to the fullest. I leave it to God's hands to call me for what He wanted me to do when the proper time comes.

I was in this state of mind when my friend Midge introduced me to Dennis, a college professor with a doctoral degree. Midge was Dennis' adjunct or assistant professor at a university in Florida. Four months after we met, he proposed to marry me, a second Dennis who proposed marriage to me. I accepted the proposal of this second Dennis and so we got engaged.

Dennis turned out to be such a wonderful intelligent, well-travelled man with whom I can discuss any subject matter in the world. I finally found my intellectual equal as partner in life. He is everything I wanted my partner to be. Like my sister Elizabeth, he too had given a hand helping the poor and the underprivileged. Instead of participating in the horrendous Vietnam War, he believed he would be of better service to humanity by joining the Peace Corps when he was twenty-two and stayed with the natives in Ethiopia for a couple of years. The headboard of our King size bed at our Master bedroom is the merged headboard and footboard of his single bed in Ethiopia, carved and colored by the native Ethiopians for him in appreciation for his services. He had quite an adventure while he was in Africa, crossing the Congo by hitchhiking to trace the path of Dr. Livingston. Three days he was on top of a banana truck riding across the Congo and five days he cruised the Congo River on barges. He also climbed Mount Kilimanjaro.

After finishing his college education, he worked as a teacher in a special education program. For four years he was a teacher of mentally handicapped children, then another four years as a teacher of mentally impaired children and another four years as a councilor for emotionally disturbed children. After finishing a doctorate degree, he became a professor at Nova Southeastern University in Florida. He is so knowledgeable about so many things that it is such a delight picking his brain!

We got married on the 7th of August 1997, seven months after we met. I am the happiest woman on earth. I have suffered so much heartache in my previous marriages to heartless partners that now I can really appreciate what a good partner Dennis is, being married to him is ecstasy beyond words. Without the anguish I went through with the wrong partners in my past, I wonder if I can fully appreciate what a truly wonderful husband Dennis is. I believe that one has to experience real deep anguish and sorrow to know the true meaning of happiness. Now I fully understand why Jesus said, "Take your cross and follow me."

I asked Dennis, "Now that I found Paradise, what will be next?" I was thinking, can this happiness last for the rest of eternity, or will it start getting boring if the happiness goes on every day? Oh well, I'll cross the bridge when I get there. I decided to put the matter aside and not to think about it anymore. I decided to savor the bliss for as long as it last and it's been almost twenty-eight years now that we had enjoyed each other in complete bliss! We have traveled every year all over the world. We have set foot on all the seven continents of earth including Antarctica. We have visited half of the National Parks in the USA and it's on our bucket list to visit all. We will keep on traveling for as long as we can to see as much as we can while we can.

Being married to Dennis means good-bye to going to church. Jesus said, "You do not need to go to the synagogue to pray, pray in secret." That's what I've been doing. Saturdays were for a good three-mile early morning walk at the boardwalk on the beach where we can enjoy the beautiful panorama of the Atlantic ocean and a movie in the afternoon or socializing with some friends or with my children who all came back home after college. It was a day just for relaxation following the Commandment Keep thou holy (Jesus told me that this means, keep your body whole and not broken up with ailments) the Sabbath day. It was a change of phase for me, but I was really thinking that it was time for me to move forward from the Seventh Day Adventist Church and explore another faith, maybe Buddhism. I felt that I have learned everything about Christianity. Sundays were for cleaning up and tidying our home and doing the laundry. It was the Romans who changed the worship day to Sunday which was the day of worship when the pagans were sun worshippers. I enjoyed sharing my feelings for God through the songs I sang during the service whenever I was invited to sing during church services but the only thing I get from the sermon of the Priest or Pastor attending Christian service is: "Listen to me, I am so eloquent, am I not? Come admire the way I speak, what a good preacher I am!"

Preachers say accept Jesus in your heart, but they don't clearly explain how. They preach salvation by faith alone, they say: You don't have to be perfect because the blood of Jesus saved you already. Does it mean you can sin all your life and at your death bed you accept Jesus and that's it, you go straight to heaven when you die? All these preachings are contrary to what Jesus said: You need to be perfect as God in heaven is perfect. Do not worship me, worship God in heaven. No one has ascended to heaven except he who came down from heaven. You need to be born again to reach the Kingdom of Heaven. I started attending Bible studics when my mind had already become so analytical that I needed more convincing interpretations. I had followed the words of Jesus since I was sixteen and had applied his philosophy in my daily life and I found them truly helpful, but the rest of the Bible is an enigma to me, I did not hear any interpretation plausible enough for me to accept until Jesus appeared to me and told me the truth.

If the words of Jesus have been successfully conveyed to the masses, how come everyone seems to be so unforgiving? America is a society of lawsuit-happy people because no one wants to forgive. Everyone wants monetary compensation for the mistake of others. What is the result of this attitude? Professionals has to obtain very costly malpractice insurance, which gives them the excuse to charge exorbitant rates for their services. Everyone ends up paying a high price for everything. I agree that this motivates competence, but it is therefore fear that motivates competence, fear of malpractice lawsuit. Can you imagine the free radicals these professionals produce in their body at the end of each working day because of the fear of getting sued for malpractice? If they are true followers of Jesus, I expect them to be forgiving people. I would rather be motivated by the fulfilling joy of a job well done so that my body will produce endorphins throughout the day. I have never asked for a salary raise from any of my employers because it is not money that motivates me to do my job well. I enjoy the daily challenges of work. It has become for me like a game, a puzzle to solve, I am a child at play and not at work when I am at the office. Fortunately, my boss was a very fair and considerate employer. I was among the highest paid employees at the time I decided to retire at age sixty-two. It was time to just relax and enjoy being with my new husband. My children were all done with college so my responsibilities as a parent were over.

I missed singing with a choir and I considered attending the nearest church from the home of Dennis, which happened to be a Catholic church but Dennis, being a professor at Nova Southeastern University, the patron of Nova Singers, a community choir in Broward County, suggested that I join the Nova Singers instead. I suddenly remembered that Susan Rust whom I sang with while we were both members of the First Baptist Church choir in Plantation was a Nova Singer soprano. It was perfect timing when I called Susan who told me that if I wanted to be a Nova Singer, that I should be at the audition the following night. It was the summer of 1997, a week after Dennis and I got married. I was very happy after taking the audition to get a call from Peggy Barber, the choir founder and director, to tell me that I passed the audition, and she told me that I would be with the second sopranos of the choir. I was given the folder number 112 and when the Christmas season came and I saw the Christmas poster came out, I realized that I was accepted to be a Nova Singer on its twenty second season. I was so delighted that two new Peggys were added to my life, one is Dennis' sister Peggy, my new sister-in-law, and Peggy the Nova Singers choir director!

A month after Dennis and I got married, I inexplicably started having nightmares that kept recurring night after night. The first time I had recurring nightmares was in 1950 when I was a six year old little girl where I was terrorized by a dream of falling from a great height in a princess dress with a skirt that opened up to be like a parachute that enabled me to float down slowly and gently to a safe landing and as soon as my feet touched the ground, my dress became the normal daily dress I wore as the child Pura. Every time this dream recurred, I did not know if it would have the same safe landing, so I went through the terror of the fall each time and it was a great relief each time it ended the same way, safely and gently. For years I had this recurring dream until 1975 when it ended. When I came to the United States in 1980, I started to have a new recurring dream. For years I dreamt of being naked in a place that was private at first and then would open up where people could see my nakedness much to my dismay.

About ten years before I married Dennis, I dreamt that I was dressed like a queen in a long voluminous dress that hampered my movements. I jumped down from a sort of an elevated platform, sort of like a balcony and I landed on a green cloud creeping on the floor, which looked exactly like that green cloud in the movie The Ten Commandments, which killed all the first born in Egypt. In my dream, this green cloud trapped both my feet firmly as I landed on the floor and my dress was transformed into my daily wear dress now in this century, as if it was a continuation of my recurring nightmares in 1950 when I was a little girl. In this dream I could move my body, but my feet were completely held in place on the floor by this low creeping green cloud. This dream woke me up terrified, but it happened only on that night and not a recurring one.

Onc night, I dreamt that I found a thick wad of money under the bench of a bus stop. I picked up this thick wad of money and as I started counting how much was my find, each piece of paper bill vanished into thin air until all had completely disappeared, I wondered if my dreams had hidden meanings. I wondered what my recurring dreams meant, but they were not really nightmares because thought they had in a way caused me some distress, they did not cause me to feel the same terror that I felt with this latest recurring dream. I asked Dennis, "I'm so happy now, why should I be having nightmares? I haven't had one for a long time until now."

In this recurring dream after I married Dennis, I saw night after night a crowd of people, stern looking, oblivious of one another, uncaring of one another, in a very busy street: they were all just walking. The vision in my dream was really nothing scary and yet there was something frightening me, but I did not know what it was. All there were people, but I woke up feeling that mankind was in some kind of great danger. This dream recurred several nights until one night I dreamt of the same scenario once again, but something was added. There was a little baby in a very pitiful condition. I saw blood on his head and his right arm was is in a position that was only possible if it was broken. Another child who seemed to be no older than ten years old was caring for this pitifully injured baby. The older child was carrying the injured infant but was unaware of his injuries while people walked around them unmindful of the pitiful condition of the two children, I woke up greatly puzzled and wondered what it meant. I was glad that these nightmares stopped shortly before Christmas.

CHAPTER 5

A t work, Dan, calls himself my platonic sidekick, a second Dan, just like Danny, my first platonic sidekick in high school. Dan said he was also Danny when he was young, he gave me a book for Christmas, The Celestine Prophecy. Two years earlier, in 1995, my youngest son gave me the exactly the same book, also as a Christmas present for me, but I was not enthusiastic on reading it because I'm not interested in prophesies concocted by a human, and I thought this was one of them. By the time I decided to read it to show my son that I appreciated what he gave me, I found out that my oldest son had lent it to a friend, and I never saw it again. The day after I received the Celestine Prophecy from Dan, I got afflicted with an infection, which needed immediate medical attention. If I made an appointment with my PCP who was always fully booked, he wouldn't see me right away so I went to the ER of a nearby hospital. I knew that going to the ER will mean hours and hours of waiting so I took the Celestine Prophesy with me. I was dealing with two builders at that time, Jack and Patty. I arranged for Jack to meet me in the ER waiting room. It was a favor for him because his construction site was nearby instead of him driving all the way to Ames Design 35 miles away. He came and handed me the truss drawings for the job which needed my approval for fabrication. I told Shane, my boss, my predicament so he went to deal with Patty himself up in Boca. The ER was so busy that it took almost the whole day before I was examined and given a prescription. The long hours of waiting gave me the time to read the Celestine Prophesy almost to the end.

I was so amazed by the contents of the book. Reading The Celestine Prophesy made me feel that the author had put into words my own experiences, the way I had felt that things were happening to educate me, the way I ate, the way I treated my children, the way I felt the signals my body organs were sending my brain, and most importantly the different insights that the author discussed. In the past I already had the hunch that there are lessons to learn from people who I came across with in my life and I already had suspected that events happened for a reason. His philosophy of drawing energy from a higher source was exactly what I had been doing, casting my burdens to Jesus. He expressed it in a more technical terminology, I expressed it in Christian terminology. His insights on humans capable of evolving into a higher state of being, capable of vibrating themselves into spirit form was exactly the same concept that I was pursuing. I was very happy to have come across another mind, which is parallel to my own. I was not alone in my quest for the impossible.

Reading this book about insights triggered memories of mysterious things that had happened to me in the past. The memory of a terrifying experience came surging into my conscious mind. It happened to me in the last three months of 1975. Dennis has a science-oriented mentality, and I didn't want to dig up anything in my past that would cause a rift in our relationship, yet I could not stop myself from sharing with him my horrific experience. I was curious how he would react to it.

I was born in the Philippines and raised as a Catholic by my parents. The Catholic Church discouraged reading the Bible. The Priest said that only those who had studied theology can read the Bible and interpret it correctly. Laymen will not understand its true meaning and will be misled, according to them. Being a very obedient parishioner, I never read the Bible. A friend, Olive, from church was carrying a little book one time entitled The Imitation of Christ. I got curious about it and Olive recommended that I should get myself one because it will be a very good guide for me to follow. I went to the local bookstore and bought myself this little book. It was small enough to carry in my purse, so I took it with me everywhere I went. My concept of the image of my God was based on the contents of this little book. Through this book Jesus became my constant companion and my imaginary friend whom I talked to, confided in, and asked help from whenever things got tough during my teenage years. I discovered that things were easier to deal with if I strictly followed the way Jesus suggested me to do. I read this little book countless times until I have digested the contents of the whole book. Its philosophy influenced every decision I made in my life.

Education changed the way I perceived things. Studying physics made me start asking, "Did God create man, or did man create God?" Although my faith had waivered, my friendship with Jesus stayed firm and strong. I had stopped regarding him as God, how can a human on earth be the God of this entire universe when earth is a minute insignificant dot viewing the entire vast universe? Anyway, he said, "Do not worship me, worship God in heaven." To me, Jesus is an exalted teacher whose philosophy is very effective in maintaining my inner peace.

Around the middle of 1975, after seven years of heartaches and disappointments from my first husband, father of my three children, I noticed a change in him. He started bringing home books written by Ruth Montgomery. "I want to know the truth" he said. He also started going out with an attractive young couple, Rey and his beautiful wife Via who always insisted to Bert to take me along on their outings. I was very grateful to these new friends whose influence on Bert looked very positive. I was hopeful that Bert would turn a new leaf. They convinced Bert to join their church, a Born-Again Christian Church. I did not hesitate to join in when they asked me. I was willing to do anything to transform Bert into a better husband and father.

The succeeding months were very calm. I thought that my marital storms were over. I was finally happy. It was during this calm that the books of Ruth Montgomery that Bert brought home caught my attention. After reading two of these books, I felt challenged by this author who claimed that she had established a connection with a spirit guide. I said to myself, "If it is true that these mysterious things could happen to her, it should happen to me too if I give it a try." The urge to find out if there was any truth to her claims was irrepressible. If a spirit would manifest to me, it would be enough proof that there is really God because God is a spirit. Ruth Montgomery advised that one must be patient at the start. She said that a friend of hers waited eight weeks before something started to happen.

I was at that time a college professor at the Mapua Institute of Technology in the Philippines teaching architectural subjects. It was October of 1975, and we were on a two weeks semestral break. Saturday, early in the morning, I got in my study room, locked the door so no one would see this crazy stunt I was about to try. I sat by my desk holding a pen over a pad of paper with eyes closed, poised for my first venture into the occult called automatic writing. I did not expect that anything would happen on my first try because Ruth Montgomery said so. I meditated deeply and to my great surprise, my hand started to move immediately before even a minute elapsed. I swear it was not my own power that made my hand move. My heart started pounding heavily as fear crept into my being. Don't be afraid, calm down, I told myself. I concentrated on making my heart to beat normally while my hand continued to scribble a note on the pad of paper. The spirit was so eager to communicate with me that it immediately jumped into action on its first opportunity to connect with me. The note scribbled by my spirit guide told me that he or she was Goodrose, my spirit guide. I enthusiastically told my younger siblings about my venture to the occult, and they asked Goodrose what it had to say to them. Goodrose responded telling each of them who they were in their previous incarnations before they were born again into their present incarnation. They didn't tell me if they believed, and they did not give me any indication that they disapproved of what I was doing. They were all brought up to respect their elders.

Monday after our semester break, at the MIT school of Architecture faculty room, I shared my venture into the occult to my fellow instructors and two of them asked me questions. The answers stunned my colleagues because Goodrose responded through the pen in my hand with answers that I couldn't have known but were convincingly accurate. I was dumbfounded, a few weeks ago, I did not believe there were spirits and there I was, fortune telling twice.

It did not take long for me to realize that what I had done had terrible consequences. What started as an exciting venture into the unknown turned out to be a most horrifying experience. I started experiencing demonic suggestions. I started to sense a sort of consciousness that was not mine, but which was trying to overcome my reasoning to take control of my being. Every time I saw a knife, or anything pointed, I felt a compelling force to stab or slash everyone in sight. I was in utmost terror. I should not have had these thoughts; I was a good person who never entertained evil thoughts before in my life. Why is this happening? I asked myself over and over.

I realized that engaging in the occult opened an access for an evil force to enter my mind and I must fight against it at all costs. I went down to my knees in deep contrition. "Oh Lord God Almighty, please forgive me for doubting your existence. I beg you to protect me from the devil who is trying to take my soul to hell!" I remorsefully implored.

The compelling urge to kill persisted. I stayed away from my kitchen to avoid the sight of knives. It was a big help that I had maids to cook for my family and me. Nights came and went without giving me any rest. A sinister force kept me awake night after night after night. I knew prolonged sleeplessness would cause chemical imbalance in my brain and I was afraid the evil force might overcome my reasoning if that happened, but I kept reminding myself that I should not panic.

One morning after one of those torturous sleepless nights, I got up exhausted. As I pushed my hair away from my face, a great force took control of both my hands, my own two hands slid down to my neck with such tremendous force and started to choke myself. I could not stop my own hands from choking me. I was aware that if fear would overcome me, I would die strangled by my own hands. So, I mustered all my courage. I knew the only way that I could fight this evil force was through my mind, so I furiously fought by mentally calling to God. "You are not merciless. You will not allow Satan to triumph over me just because I doubted your existence. I implore you to please release my hands from the clutches of this devil." I was greatly relieved when my hands were released, and I was full of gratitude to God for hearing my plea. I indignantly told Satan, "I will overcome you; I am not evil. I have been good all my life and you are not going to take me; my God will not allow you to have power over me!"

As soon as my hands were freed, I dressed and ran to church to give thanks. I thought I would be closer to God if I were in church. I had stopped the practice of going to church ever since I started to be a skeptic. It was still very early in the morning. I saw a few young men, the altar boys, preparing the altar for the 6:00AM mass. I knelt down in deep prayers but when I looked up to the life size statue of a saint next to me, I saw him glaring down at me with an evil eye and an evil grin. I looked at another sculpted image and it too was looking down at me in the same evil manner. I looked around at all the images, one after another. They were everywhere inside the church, and to my horror, they were all looking at me with an evil eye and an evil grin, even the image of the crucified Christ and the image of his mother Mary.

This can't be happening, not in your house dear God, not in your house! was my silent indignant cry in great disbelief. But alas! it was happening. I ran out of the church as fast as I could. I ran back home and started searching for the Bible. I had bought a Bible but had not had the chance to read it. I searched in great haste while my brain was full of questions of why the incident at the church happened. I found the book and opened it. The first thing that my eyes gazed upon was the verse, which read, "God dwells not in temples made by hands." Although my whole being was in a state of terror, I did not fail to notice how amazing it was that the Bible opened to the exact answer to my question. I did not even have to search. I held the Bible close to my chest and continued to ask, why are all these things happening, dear God, why? I opened the Bible once again and my eyes came upon the verse, which read, "Thou shalt not invoke spirits." Forgive me dear God, forgive me, I did not know. I fervently prayed. Once again, the Bible gave me an answer without the need to search, but my amazement got lost in my apprehension over the whole horror-filled events that had just unfolded.

The bible became my weapon against Satan. It came to life for me. Every time I had a question, I opened the book exactly to the page where the answer was, and my eyes gazed at exactly the right passage I needed to read. When fear started to overcome me, I opened the book, and I found the appropriate verse that gave me the encouragement I needed. The words of Jesus gave me so much strength. Jesus helped me fight Satan through the Bible. As I read his words, it seemed that the texts jumped out of the page and the sensation that I experienced was more of hearing rather than reading. It was as if Jesus was speaking right next to me. I was greatly comforted.

Satan was persistent. He was determined to convert me into a murderer. He continued to torment me relentlessly. One night I carried my sleeping youngest son who was three years old at that time, up the stairs to put him to bed when Satan suddenly urged me to drop my baby just before I got to the uppermost step. I felt my arms getting limp compelling me to do what he bade me to do. I held my baby closer to me and ran up the last steps as fast as I could. It was horrendous! The relentless urgings of Satan tormented me so gravely that there is no word that can describe enough the horror I went through during those days.

I repeatedly implored God Almighty's mercy to release me from Satan's wicked taunting. Then one day, while I was in deep prayer, I suddenly heard a thundering voice speaking with great authority, "I am the Lord God Almighty who had spoken to Abraham." I was amazed and shocked at what I heard! God had come to deliver me from Satan! I thought. I could not believe that God Himself came to the summons of a nobody like me, but at the same time, I was greatly relieved that he had come to save me. The voice commanded me to get a pen and paper to write what he had to say. I was so very eager to obey. I could not find a pen but I found a pencil. The Lord God Almighty dictated a lengthy message that filled the whole page of a lined yellow paper. I obediently followed everything that he bade me to do. He asked me to take his message to the local newspaper and to have it published. I immediately carried out the errand I was told to do. At the newspaper office, I approached the man at the front desk and explained to him my task and that God himself had spoken to me. The man at the front desk did not say a word but looked at me with the expression on his face that read like, "You poor lady, you need psychiatric help." I tried to explain to him the urgency of my task but he continued to say nothing and just kept looking at me with so much pity in his eyes.

I left the newspaper office dejected and asked God Almighty what to do next since the man apparently did not believe me. He bade me to mail his message to Prince Charles. He said that this young future monarch would be a good mediator to get his message known to the world. I obeyed. I put his message in an envelope and wrote on the envelope, Prince Charles, England. I did not know his address. I went to the post office and paid the required fee and mailed it.

God Almighty sent me to the park close by several times with the promise of making an apparition. I obediently followed because I wanted to see God so badly. On one of my trips to the park, I saw a patch of clover alongside the road and it struck me that they had four leaves. I remembered hearing a story about the good luck that comes to one who finds a four-leaf clover, so I bent down to pluck one for souvenir, but then I noticed that the whole patch had four leaves, and they were everywhere along the road growing wildly just like any weed. So I thought, what is so special about a four-leaf clover when it appears to be just another weed species growing in such abundance? I dismissed the idea of plucking one for keepsake, thinking that perhaps in Ireland this species was rare, but it did not seem that way in the Philippines. So I continued my walk to the park and did not bother anymore to pick not even one of the four-leaf clover. Each time I got to the park, I would wait for hours and hours for God Almighty to appear, but He never did, much to my disappointment. However, He kept talking to me. Finally, he announced that I had passed all the tests and that I should go Luneta Park where a throng of people were waiting to witness my proclamation as queen of hearts. I put on my favorite dress and went to Luneta Park where I found many people just relaxing, doing their own thing completely oblivious of my presence. God Almighty bade me to walk to the middle of the grassy mall and then said, "Now announce to everyone on top of your voice that you, the queen of hearts, has come so that they would come to adore you!"

Jesus' words from my little book suddenly flashed to my mind, "Humble yourself before God and He will lift you up." So I asked God Almighty, "If you are my true God, please do the announcing so that they would believe." A deafening silence followed. God Almighty did not respond. I then realized that this voice that has tricked me into believing that he was Lord God Almighty, was a fake god. I told him in defiance, "Go away from me! You are not my God!" I went home feeling so indignant and horribly disappointed to realize that my war against Satan was not over yet.

If this had happened to anyone else, if one suddenly heard a voice saying, "I am the Lord God Almighty!" Would he not believe? This is what happened in Genesis 22;2 and Deuteronomy 20;16 and they believed. I am not the only one so gullible to believe Satan's deception.

On several more occasions, Satan tried to kill me, but I fought back and had overcome him. After his failed attempts to kill me physically, he started attacking my sanity and his deception as Lord God Almighty was his first attempt. He continued to torture my sanity with the voices of people, some I knew personally, many I didn't. I heard voices day and night nonstop. It was like being a telepath who could hear the thoughts of everyone, but they are unpleasant thoughts, which I did not want to hear. It was sheer torture.

One day, I sat down and read the Bible aloud to take my mind away from the voices. For no reason at all, I chose to read Revelation aloud. It was so strange that while I was reading, visions came to my mind seemingly illustrating the meaning of what I was reading. I saw the visions of the apparition of Mary at Lourdes, and it was befuddling that the passages were telling me that this was how the dragon that was cast into the earth persecuted the woman who brought forth the man child. The vision told me that the phenomenon of Mary's apparition was not from God, I was greatly shocked by the vision I saw when I was reading about the great Harlot of Babylon.

Another showed me that the first thousand years that Satan was held in the bottomless pit was the first millennium after the crucifixion of Christ. I saw visions of the early Christian churches that I had studied in the history of architecture, the Dark Ages, when people burned all books and turned away from all kinds of learning and all their aspirations were focused on spirituality or matters of the soul. At the end of the first thousand years, under Charlemagne's leadership, people gradually started to read and write again, and they rediscovered learning. The passages in the Revelation also said that this is the first resurrection.

As I was reading the passages about the next thousand years when Satan was released on Earth to deceive men once more, the vision I saw were the images of the Renaissance, the second millennia. Also, this is the second resurrection. As I read about the Island of Patmos, I saw visions of the peninsula of the island of Luzon, where I was born. What in the world did that mean? Why did the vision tell me that Patmos was the island of my birth?

I read the entire Book of Revelation aloud, and the visions I saw were all a puzzle to me, but they became clearer as my communion with the Supreme Power Above progressed. I am rewriting this manuscript today because a publisher offered to re-publish this book – The Book of life - that was originally published in the year 2000 by Vantage Press, which has already gone out of business. I cannot find my original manuscript, so I am retyping the whole book after I wrote the original more than a quarter of a century ago. I was not aware of the full magnitude of my task when I wrote this book for the first time right after God spoke to me while Dennis and I were touring the Mayan temples in Merida. I have written two other books after the Supreme Power Above laid on my shoulders the full magnitude of my task which is to eradicate all false beliefs caused by manifestations of archetypes emanating from our collective unconscious created by false beliefs, unveiling the identities of false prophets and false gods.

Let me continue the manuscript of my original book – The Book of Life. While I was going through my ordeal with Satan, who is actually the manifestation of what Dr, Carl Gustav Jung perceived as the negative dynamic archetype that emanates from our collective unconscious, I saw more visions not related to the Bible. I saw the vision of the Greek goddess Hera, which was a puzzle to me at that time, and I also heard the voices identifying themselves as Sigmund Freud and Albert Einstein. I kept hearing them, but I could not properly connect with them to make any sense of what they were trying to convey to me at that time. I asked my sister Elizabeth over and over if Freud or Einstein were still alive because I did not know if the voices trying to connect with me were voices of the dead or the living. It was a big puzzle for me at that time.

My ordeal with Satan ended on New Year's Eve. The three long arduous months of fighting for my life and my sanity finally came to an end, They were the three longest months of my life. My life went back to normal, thank God. My encounter with the devil confirmed the existence of Satan without any more doubts in my mind. Every time senseless mass killings are headline news; I am reminded of my ordeal and I know that the killer was possessed by Satan. If I can overcome Satan, there is no excuse for anyone not to do the same.

Every time I shared my story to people I trusted; I left out the seemingly irrelevant visions of the Greek goddess and Einstein and Freud's voices because I didn't want anyone suspecting that I have lost my sanity. I thought it was delightful to see the clear vision of Benjamin Franklin flying a kite on a stormy thunderous day with lightnings flashing dangerously in the skies, while a busy body, who could be Hermes or an angel, fluttered to and fro, propping things up to help him discover electricity. It was telling me that the Supreme Power Above aided Man's scientific discoveries. Of course, I would not ever tell any Catholic that I saw visions of Mary's apparitions with a message that it was the manifestations of archetypes emanating from our collective unconscious created by repeated prayers (the rosary) and worshipping the image of Mary, which is a violation of the first Commandment handed down to Moses forbidding worship of any image from heaven, earth or seas. Although if they cannot accept this truth, they will not attain the purity of mind required to reach perfection.

I know I have overcome the power of Satan through the power of my true God in Heaven because my strength had failed me in the end, and I gave up to Satan. It was when I gave up the fight that the true God took over. He gave me a very clear sign, which assured me that it was my friend Jesus who had come to help me. He did not allow Satan to take my life nor my soul. I lost my last battle with Satan, but I won the war. After this harrowing ordeal with the Antichrist, I never called on God Almighty again. I realized that calling God with praises makes the vain man-made god come. Since then, I call only the Supreme Power Above, which I shorten to SPA. On the letter of Jesus to the church in Pergamus, he said – to one who overcomes shall be given a white stone with a new name. After my encounter with the SPA at Merida, I found a white stone with the letters SPA naturally inscribed in it formed by tiny organisms, believe it or not.

A couple of months after I mailed to Prince Charles the letter dictated to me by the false god almighty who was Satan in disguise who was trying to embarrass me to insanity, I received a very elegant card with a note from His Royal Highness Prince Charles, thanking me for sending him a letter. I was so embarrassed to realize that he had received the message from the false god, which I sent him. I had hoped that it had gotten lost in the mail because I did not know the address. I consoled myself with the thought that his secretary would not bother him with a letter of insanity. In my embarrassment, I immediately trashed the elegant card so it would not be a reminder of my ordeal with Satan. Later, I learned that I'm not the only one duped by Beelzebub to do stupid things. The Bible spoke of a prophet who ate the whole scroll of scriptures and another one who walked the streets stark naked.

I lost my post as instructor at the university. I could not function normally during my three-month ordeal, and I was concerned for the safety of my students. If I lost my war against Satan, my innocent students might have been the victims, and my name would have been on top of the list of senseless school mass killers. I regret that I had left my post the way I did, I went AWOL, but there was no way I could explain what I was going through to the Dean of Architecture and Planning at MIT Philippines even though he was my friend.

On my subsequent strolls to the park, I noticed that the four-leaf clovers that were growing so profusely on the roadside had disappeared completely, and I have never seen any four-leaf clovers again ever.

After listening to my horror story, the only thing Dennis asked me was if those urgings to kill ever recurred. I assured him they never did. Judging from his reaction, I knew he was among those who dismiss experiences like mine as the creation of someone's mind, a malfunction of the brain sort of. I shared this story to Kathleen Raskin, my therapist, during the time I was still having sessions with her. I wanted to know how a present-day psychotherapist would think about it. I was happy with her reply. "There are many things that happen that we cannot explain," she said. I had shared this story to a few people whom I trusted, hoping to find a reason why, after I had followed my little book to the letter, I was still vulnerable to the ploys of Satan, but was I vulnerable? Satan failed to turn me into a senseless murderer. Despite the horrifying encounter with the evil force, I have no regrets that I went through the ordeal, it was a learning process for me. It had proven to me without any more doubt that God truly exists, and my faith became solid as a rock since then. It also proved to me that Satan is alive and well causing havoc to mankind.

After this ordeal with Satan, the whisper in the wind came to me again more pronounced than before. One time while I was with the First Baptist Choir during a Sunday service singing the Beatitudes, when we got to the part, Blessed are the pure in heart for they shall see God, I was startled when suddenly I heard, "That's why you had seen God," whispered in my ears. I have a pure heart? I wasn't aware I have a pure heart. After a year, our choir director chose me to sing the "Song of Mary" during church service. Towards the end of my song, I heard, "You are singing your song," whispered in my ears, which startled me that I missed a note. Luckily, Cal, our illustrious pianist, expertly ad-libbed to camouflage my mishap. What in the world did it mean? I was so puzzled, and I couldn't think of any reason why and how Mary's song could be my song, I thought I did not hear what was whispered to me correctly.

One time, I was driving home from work with a heavy heart. I was feeling so low that day. It was that time when I received the news that my beloved father had passed away. It felt like my security wall had crumbled away. It was then that I realized how my father had given me that feeling of security knowing where I could always run back to and find refuge if a catastrophe happened and now it's gone, making me so forlorn. Suddenly my feeling of misery miraculously turned into a feeling of overwhelming joy. I said, "Oh dear Supreme Power Above, so this is what you mean by blessed are they who mourn for they shall be comforted. That made me feel lighter for the rest of the day and it hastened the end of my grief. Then again, as I was driving home from work, I heard a voice, this time it was not a whisper, saying, "You are the chosen one." I instantaneously replied, "Chosen to do what?" I already got used to hearing whispers in the wind by that time so I jokingly said, "Well, if you want me to be your spokesperson, I would greatly be honored, but you have to put words in my mouth because I wouldn't know what to say, in fact, if that position is not yet filled, I would like to apply for it." That would be a very good purpose for my life. Hearing whispers in the wind had happened repeatedly in my life since I was a little girl that to me it had become commonplace, so I just forget about them right after they happen. I never told anyone about it because I am sure people would think that I am weird if I claim to be having these kinds of experiences.

While I was reading the Celestine Prophesy, the whisper in my ear told me that the message is from Heaven. It was Celestial. The vision of John the Baptist preparing the way for Jesus also kept creeping in my mind. I was so puzzled as to why I was having those visions. When I came to the part of the book saying that a highly evolved person would come to show the way, the whisper in the wind told me that I was that person. That really gave me goosebumps. Why is this happening? I kept asking myself. I was stupefied by what's going on. The Celestine Prophesy said that things happen for a reason, Did I get that infection that sent me to the ER so that I could read the Celestine Prophesy before Christmas? The whisper in my ear also started urging me to look into the meaning of my name and to write my story. I knew I was a witness to both the SPA and Satan. Is that what I needed to write about? But I did not know how to write. I am an Architect trained to express my ideas graphically not literally. What about my name? What is in my name?

Late on Christmas night, after all festivities and celebrations were over, before going to bed, I packed a few clothes in a small suitcase for the trip to Mexico that Dennis and I planned to take the following morning. It was our four-months delayed honeymoon. We were both still working and our work duties did not allow us to have a honeymoon vacation when we got married last August. While I was already in bed trying to get some sleep, something very strange once again happened. I was once again dressed in a queenly garb as if a continuation of my dream when I jumped down from a high platform and my feet were caught by a green colored cloud creeping low on the floor. This time, I was told I was Queen Catherine of Aragon, and I was at the tower of London, I saw massive masonry walls with glass panes on windows and then a huge antique key dropped by my feet making a cling-clang sound on the concrete floor but I was aware that I was in my bedroom that was fully carpeted. It was like being half asleep dreaming and half awake. When I originally wrote about this in my first book when I was 54 years old, I did not have the courage to give these details fearing ridicule but now that I am 80 years old, I don't care anymore. This was what truly happened. Right after that, I must have gone into deep slumber because the next thing I knew, it was morning and it was time to get up. Dennis and I had a plane to catch, and the hectic schedule of the day made me forget the strange happening of the previous night.

It was December 26, 1997, when Dennis and I arrived at Merida, Mexico to see the temples Uxmal and Chichen Itza. Dennis was a bit annoyed because our luggage was not on the plane with us. It was for me an excuse to go shopping, which for sure I was going to enjoy so it did not bother me. The airport personnel assured us that our luggage will arrive on the next incoming flight from Miami, scheduled the next day. It meant we did not have our toiletries and change of clothing for the night and the following day. At the hotel where we had our reservations, a porter took us to a room that was not cleaned yet. We had to go back to the front desk to get another room. When our room problem got settled, we took a walk to the nearest shopping center to buy what we needed for the night and the following day. We ended up buying two of everything, toothbrushes, underwear, shorts, tops, everything. The only item that we bought in the singular was the contact lens cleaner, yet we had to go back to the store to buy another one because it was the wrong cleaner, all the labeling were in Spanish, Dennis only found out when he opened the packaging.

The hotel room we got was so close to the air conditioners that we could hear the machines throughout the night, so we requested another change of room a second time. We finally got settled in room 102. Our patience was under trial, everything went wrong on our first day in Merida. To top that, we woke up the following morning and peaked out of the window to see a dreary rainy day. I saw Dennis' face drooped in disappointment, so I cajoled him saying, "Well dear husband, it seems like we are being tested to prove how evolved we are. If we allow these minor mishaps ruin our vacation, it will mean we are not evolved enough, but if we enjoy ourselves in spite of everything, then we are indeed highly evolved beings." I was glad he took the challenge in good spirits.

There was no abating of the rain when we got to the site of the Mayan temples. We did not expect that it would be so cold and wet, so we did not consider buying sweaters and raincoats when we went shopping the previous night. I was miserably cold as I was getting drenched with rain while following the tour guide who was relating to the whole tour group the whole story about the Mayan temples. I suddenly remembered stories of people walking on live burning coal and survival stories of people who were trapped in icy cold water in Alaska in winter for hours and hours and yet survived. So, I tried mind over matter game, telling myself, if those people could do it, I could do it too. I suggested to myself to burn my unwanted body fat to warm me up and at the same time lose some extra weight. Believe it or not, it worked and despite the rain, for the rest of that cold dreary day, although I was wet, I was comfortably warm while following the tour guide and happily toured the ruins going up and down the pyramids.

I gazed at the pyramid in awe, trying to analyze the Mayan building techniques. I was telling myself, what a magnificent monument of man's endeavor to reach God. I was thinking of the bloody human sacrifice as part of the worship rites that the Mayan priests performed when suddenly, I was startled by visions that flooded my mind followed by telepathic messages. The visions suddenly popped out in my mind unexpectedly just as I had experienced twenty-two years ago.

My brain started receiving visions from somewhere. It was as if my brain had become a receiver of a telecast from Heaven. The frequency of my brain's vibration must have gotten synchronized with that of heaven so that I started receiving its transmissions. The Supreme Power Above played a symphony of messages, using my brain as a keyboard. He touched a specific point in my brain to activate a resurgence of a memory of specific acquired knowledge, which did not mean much to my mortal perception, but when the SPA activated these bits and pieces of information in proper sequence, it created a message he intended me to recognize. The fake God Almighty spoke to me with words spoken like a human, but the SPA spoke in visions and telepathy. He evoked my emotions to confirm if I understood his message correctly or not. I felt assured when I understood him correctly and I felt lost and doubtful when I did not comprehend His message accurately. It was then that I realized that the whispers in the wind were his way of teaching me His language since I was a little girl. But it was only then that I learned to fully understand Him.

The first vision I saw was the Biblical scene of Abraham as he raised his hand holding a dagger so slaughter his son to offer as sacrifice to his god and then the angel came to stop him. The vision came with a telepathic message that the SPA did not ask Abraham to slaughter his own son. It was the SPA who sent the angel to stop Abraham from killing his son. Instantly, another vision followed. When I first wrote about this second vision I saw, in my original book twenty-five years ago, I thought god was sending the Children of Israel to war with the telepathic message that it was not the SPA commanding men to go to war. On my subsequent communications with the SPA, I realized that the vision I saw was that this false god sent the Children of Israel to commit genocide wiping out six tribes. Right after these two powerful visions, the image of the god almighty who sent me to idiotic tasks to embarrass me to insanity in 1975 twenty-two years ago, flashed in my mind. The SPA confirmed to me that the god who told Abraham to kill his son written in Genesis 22;2, the god who told the children of Israel to commit genocide written in Deuteronomy 20;16 was the same false god who spoke to me twenty-two years ago. The false god almighty told me that he was the god who spoke to Abraham. I can imagine that the authoritative commanding voice I heard claiming to be my

Lord God Almighty was the same voice Abraham heard and also what the children of Israel heard more than four thousand years ago. I was not the only one deceived by Satan. This false god is the same as the god of the Mayans that demanded human sacrifice. I was appalled by these revelations revealed to me. I wondered, is that how powerful the fake god was that he was written in the Bible as God? The passage in the Bible saying - God dwells not in temples made my hands - flashed into my mind with telepathic confirmation that these are the true words of the SPA. Then the passage in the Bible about God giving the specifications for the Arc of the Covenant and the Tabernacle flashed in my mind with telepathic message that the SPA did not require the building of the Tabernacle nor any item of worship.

My encounter with the SPA at the site of the Mayan temples had confirmed that the visions that were shown to me while I read the Revelation twenty-two years ago while I was going through my ordeal with Satan were the truth. I could not believe what was happening to me, and I wondered, was this what the Buddhists call reaching Buddhahood? I must have indeed reached Paradise, and it is true that in Paradise, you commune with the SPA! I knew then why Buddha said that God is within us because the SPA was communicating with me from within.

I am a divorced woman who remarried, and yet the SPA communed with me, therefore what I had done was not offensive to Him. When I joined the Baptist church and then the Seventh Day Adventist Churches, I was condoned by the Pastors from the sin of adultery because my previous spouses had sexual intimacy with other women outside of marriage. I was happy but then, the fact that I had stopped going to church came to my mind, so I asked the SPA, "I stopped going to church on Sabbath, doesn't that make me a sinner?" (Please understand that my communication with the SPA was telepathic but I am imparting it to you literally) He asked me, "What do you do on Sabbath?" I responded, "I relax and keep myself physically and mentally fit." His response was, "You keep yourself whole." "Yes, dear SPA, "I replied."

The Commandment – Thou keep holy the Sabbath day suddenly flashed into my mind fully enlightened of what it truly meant. "Dear

SPA, You mean, keep our body whole?" Then it dawned on me, how does one keep holy in the first place? Who is the judge if one is holy? Oh jubilation, I am okay then, I did not sin when I stopped going to church. This was confirmed by Jesus who said, " You do not need to go to the synagogue to pray, pray in secret."

There was a time when I felt I was abandoned by God after my quest to do nothing but good was rewarded by devastating marriages. In my frustration, I became vulnerable to experiment on finding out how it was to be a woman of the sexual revolution for just once in my life. I asked the SPA, If He would condone me for that too? He asked, "Were you committed to someone when you did it?" I replied, "No." He asked, "Was he committed to anyone?" I replied, "No." "Did you hurt anyone?" He asked. I replied, "No." "Then what is your sin?" My whole life cycle was flashed before me. I told the SPA, "Well dear SPA, you know my life very well and if you say I did not sin, then I have no sin."

The SPA went over the Ten Commandments with me one by one and told me what each one of them meant. He confirmed that we are programmed to self-destruct when we sin. Our body produce death agents that attack our immune system making us susceptible to diseases that can kill us. The Commandments were given to us to follow to prevent the activation of the self-destruct program and if we knowingly choose to break them, then we suffer the consequence. Our body produces the death agents that would slowly kill us until our physical body dies. Jesus said that one who does not follow even the least of his Commandment is not worthy of him, and he refers to himself because he is life. Therefore, one who breaks even the least of his commandments is not worthy of life.

I realized that it was the SPA who had been guiding me to the path towards finding the truth. It was He who was speaking to me whenever I heard the voice in the wind. We indeed need to be perfect to be able to join the SPA in that highest level of existence as an omnipotent being who does not die a physical death. We indeed need to become angels to reach the kingdom of God. I then realized that the serpent in the story of Adam and Eve who said that if you eat of the fruit of knowledge, you would become God as the voice of truth. Whoever had received this message from the SPA reacted just like I did when the SPA showed me visions of truth, which I could not accept because they were contrary to my religious indoctrination when I was a child.

I have not said the rosary after overcoming my ordeal with Satan and there was a time that I tried to recite the Nicene Creed, but I forgot it already. That evening at Merida, I suddenly found myself reciting it from start to finish, remembering every word of it. The SPA pointed out what was wrong with it. "Do you see what the Christians do to Jesus?"

"Yes, dear SPA, they made him sit at the right hand of God, the Father Almighty. Dear SPA, Christians are not aware that God Almighty is not you."

"I don't need any praises of any kind; I am not a vain God. When you chant praises to God, you create a vain god."

At the part of the Nicene Creed that said, "I believe in the resurrection of the dead," the SPA asked, "Do you understand what that means?" "I do not know what resurrection means," I replied." "Do you believe that you will not die if you believe in the words of Jesus?" "That is what the Scriptures say, and you know that I am trying to prove it to be literally true." "You have found the truth." "You mean I will be omnipotent like Q if I reach that ultimate purity of mind, body and soul?" "Yes." He replied. I asked, "If I have found the truth, what happened then to those who led good lives and yet died, since I have not heard of anyone who has reached immortality?" He replied, "What did the Scriptures say?" The words of Jesus flashed in my mind, "You need to be born again to reach the Kingdom of Heaven." "You mean that we reincarnate? Is that what born again means, to reincarnate?" I asked. "You have found the truth." He replied.

I was about to ask why was it that when Nicodemus asked Jesus if to be born again meant to come out from a mother's womb, his reply was in an indirect manner that was vague, which led to the Christian interpretation as to be born again in a baptismal ritual. Then visions of the caste system in Hindu society where men were not born equal being the human early response to the Avatar's clear doctrine of reincarnation flashed in my mind and everything became very clear to me.

Please understand that the communion I had with the SPA was

visions, mental telepathy, feelings and emotions, which I translated into verbal form the best way I could, to convey to you the context of our communication.

The English language forces me to refer to the SPA with a gender when the truth is that the SPA has no gender, He is without a name, without a form, He is pure all-knowing spirit energy. At this point, I really had a dilemma as to how to convey what had happened in sequence because I am so inexperienced in storytelling. Please allow me to continue my story not in the proper order of sequence in which events happened because this is the only way I know how to clearly express myself. I understood what the SPA conveyed to me about who Satan is but I did not possess the terminology to express it.

While Dennis and I were at the Mayan ruins together with other tourists, I could no longer focus my attention on the tour guide who was relating to us stories about the Mayans who built the temples. I was completely absorbed by my communion with the SPA. At the tour bus, I tried to tell Dennis what was going on with me, "Dear, what would you say if some truths were revealed to me today?" Although he was polite in his reply, it was very apparent that he was a skeptic, who like most people dismissed this kind of phenomenon I was experiencing as a trick of the mind. It is very frustrating to know something is happening and knowing that no one would believe it. I realized I had to be very cautious not to ruin my new marriage.

Four months quickly went by after we came back to our home in Florida from our trip to the Mayan temples. I tried to share my paranormal experiences with Dennis but being strongly science oriented, who needs physical evidence of any claim before he would believe, he had remained the steadfast skeptic. My problem was that I could visualize what the SPA conveyed to me but I did not have the proper words to express it. I did not know how to call it. I knew it had something to do with manifestations of people's collective beliefs, fears and fantasies, but I did not have the accepted terminology to convey it. However, one time, in one of our discussions, he told me about Dr. Carl Gustav Jung's theory of the collective unconscious. I was thrilled by the possibility of finding a well-known psychoanalyst as an ally.

On Good Friday, I went to the bookstore looking for a book by

Jung. I browsed through some of his books, but they were all too highly technical for me to comprehend. It was such a great jubilation for me when amidst these highly technical books on psychoanalysis, my search was rewarded when I found the Simplified Jung for Beginners by Jon Platania. It was so easy to comprehend and had very delightful, comical illustrations. Oh thank you, thank you Jon! I know you purposely created this book to educate me about Jung.

I learned that the famous and at the same time infamous psychoanalyst also lost his faith and just like me, searched for the truth. In his search, he managed to tap into a higher source of knowledge, and he was given insight into the phenomenon of the collective unconscious of man. Unfortunately, he did not possess the moral strength to overcome the energy of the collective unconscious when its negative forces seduced him and he himself committed great blunders. Satan was wise, he knew that the best way to eliminate an adversary is to turn him into an ally. The Satan seduced Her Jung became a womanizer and a Nazi analyst of the Third Reich. He equated the Christ and the Antichrist as one and the same being both the result of men's unconscious. Christians branded Herr C.G. Jung a blasphemer and his great accomplishment of perceiving the collective unconscious was pushed aside as unworthy of attention of all man. Satan's vulnerability was camouflaged. Satan, who is the Antichrist, knew too well that man's acknowledgement of the collective unconscious would be his Waterloo.

Suddenly, I found the correct terminology to express what the SPA had been trying to convey to me for the past twenty-two years. Everything that I had experienced, the force that took control of my own hands to strangle me to death, the force that tried to overcome my reasoning to possess me, the demonic suggestions that tried to make me grab a knife to slaughter everyone in sight were the forces of the negative dynamic archetype that emanated from our collective unconscious created by collective thoughts that are evil, perverse, superstitious, destructive and all negative thoughts, which is parallel to the dark side of the force as in Star Wars, a force we call Satan or Beelzebub in the Bible. The SPA tried to convey to me that collective beliefs in deities make these deities manifest. That was the purpose of giving me the vision of the goddess Hera, Greco-Roman literature is full of stories of the manifestations of their deities resulting from their idolatry. Sigmund Freud was the father of psychoanalysis and C.G. Jung was his successor. The SPA was urging me to look into their query on psychoanalysis because it is the key to the puzzle of these paranormal phenomena. I had known Carl Gustav Jung only by name. I did not know his work until that Good Friday when I found his simplified book that I read in its entirety to learn about his theory of the collective unconscious. When my sister Elizabeth was studying to be a doctor, her books on Freud attracted me and have read some of his works. The SPA was trying to use Freud to lead me to Jung, but it took more than twenty-two years for me to get the whole picture. Benjamin Franklin and Albert Einstein were the clues to the fact that everything that is happening has a scientific explanation.

Who really is Satan, or Beelzebub, or the Devil? When the SPA gave me clues to the nature of Satan in the last three months of 1975 with visions and voices, my intelligence was still lacking to fully comprehend His message, which is written in the Bible as: By hearing they shall hear and shall not understand; and seeing they shall see and shall not perceive. He gave me more clues to the nature of Satan this second time and that was when I finally saw the full picture of what He had been trying to convey to me. It took twenty-two more years of enriching my mind with more knowledge of man's developments before His message became very clear. I did not know that enriching my mind with more knowledge was what was needed to reach the SPA again. In fact, I was not trying to reach Him at all. I though that because I had freed myself from all restrictions and requirements of all religions, I had made myself ineligible to reach Him. I took the attitude of just letting my conscience be my guide, appeasing myself with the thought that for as long as I was not knowingly hurting or causing anyone to be unhappy, I was not committing sin. I just happened to have an unquenchable thirst for knowledge. My encounter with the SPA a second time was a complete surprise.

The collective unconscious of man encompasses beliefs, fears and apprehensions of a society as a whole, In the seventies, the minds of man were focused on the subject of evil possession. Movie makers saturated the minds of man with stories of evil possessions, exorcisms and poltergeist. I saw the first Exorcist movie and I did not like it. Watching horror movies is not entertaining for me. Although I stayed away from these horror movies, I still became an unwilling target of the negative dynamic energy created by the collective unconscious of man. It happened to me despite following Jesus faithfully because I engaged in the occult activity of automatic writing. This is the reason the SPA forbids invoking spirits because it makes one vulnerable to the negative forces of the collective unconscious. At the time it happened to me, I perceived Satan as an evil force doing everything in his power to corrupt man. My experience was very real. Satan's manifestations were very real. I sympathize with all people who have undergone alien abduction experiences when the attention of man was held by stories such as Star Wars, Star Trek, X Files, etc. I know that just like my own experience with the devil, their experience with aliens were also very real, but these phenomena are the manifestations of the archetypes emanating from the collective unconscious created by the apprehensions of man, which at that time was the fear of aliens.

When Emperor Constantine embraced Christianity and made it the religion of the state, the Roman priests did not change their way of worship. All they did was change the deity to worship. They simply replaced Jupiter with Jesus, Juno, Jupiter's wife with Mary, mother of Jesus and the minor gods with the saints but the pagan worship rites were carried on and the Christian Orthodox Church was born. They continued their practice of saying litanies of praises to the deity worshipped that evolved into the rosary, ignoring what Jesus said – Do not say repeated prayers. They ignored the original first Commandment handed down to Moses by the SPA that forbids the worship of any image from heaven, earth and seas and edited it to – Thou shalt not worship any graven images before me – and any image of Jesus, Mary and the Saints were not graven images. They continued the practice of creating the images of the deities in sculpted marble, or mosaic, or paintings, which were then images of Jesus with a golden crown ignoring the advice of Jesus to give up all your material possessions, or Mary and images of all other saints, which in fact is what idolatry is.

At the Vatican, the Roman Catholic Church was born with Christ as the major deity, and the theatrical pagan worship rituals were carried out as it were when they were still worshipping their god Jupiter, with the burning of incense, ringing of the bells, etc. The pompous attire of the Roman high Priest became the bejeweled attire of the Pope, and all the glorious fanfares of worship that originated in the pagan Roman religious rituals continue to this day.

Greco-Roman literatures are full of tales of their gods interfering with human activities because apparition of deities are the result of collective idolatry and repeated prayers. Today, hundreds of reports of the apparition of Mary or the Lady in white are in the Vatican. Apparitions of Jesus created religions such as the Shakers' religion and the Mormons' Church of the Later Day Saints religion that cannot give up man's patriarchal role in society and women are subjugated. I am a woman to whom the SPA made these revelations of truth, this must be the SPA's means of showing that man and woman are equal.

Catholics had made devotions to Mary, the mother of Jesus, and after two thousand years of saying repeated prayers to her image, hundreds of visual manifestations of her image had been reported. To me this is no different from the manifestations of images of unidentified flying objects or UFO because of the collective attention to imagined alien visitations provoked by collective fascination to the prevailing subject of man's imagined intergalactic expeditions such as The War of the Worlds, Star Wars, Star Trek, etc. There was a prankster who created a fake photograph of the Loch Ness monster that captured the attention of the masses. Even after the admission of this prankster that his photo was a prank, and after a thorough observation of the lake using the most modern scanning equipment failed to confirm the existence of this feared monster, reports of the sightings of a monster at Loch Ness continues.

Satan the Antichrist is the negative dynamic archetype that emanates from the collective unconscious of man. He is alive and well and is enjoying his state of being and would not want to be put away. Man had been writing about manifestations of archetypes ever since he learned to write, many written as manifestation of God, which in fact were Satan in disguise. The tale of Lucifer and his minions where they were cast out of heaven came to my mind, was this the start of what science calls – The Big Bang – that started this physical universe 13.8 billion years ago? Have you ever wondered why almost all ancient religions were human sacrificing religions? The SPA planted the seed of life on earth, which is one of the visions I saw as the SPA enlightened me of the truth. I saw visions that told me that the ultimate purpose of life is to turn matter back to pure energy to be one with the SPA back in heaven in eternal life, which was what Jesus accomplished, and Jesus said, come and follow me. There is physical evidence in his shroud that Jesus did not die, he metamorphosed body and soul to be one with the SPA in eternal life. It appears that Lucifer wants to maintain this physical universe that he is aspiring to take full control of, and he is doing everything in his power to prevent us from attaining the ultimate purpose of life. He wants us all to be evil and evil thoughts create Satan, his general, to possess the morally bankrupt and mentally impaired to become senseless murderers that will become particles of physical matter devoid of life, dead forever. The SPA showed me that the observation of the scientists Higgs and Boson where they saw energy turning into particle of matter is the meaning of the Biblical passage – sinner soul cast to the lake of fire. I saw that the energy of an irredeemable soul turns into a particle of lava that is spewed out by a volcanic eruption, thus written in the Bible as sinner soul cast to the lake of fire, meaning the termination of life that the SPA planted on earth. Lucifer started all the human sacrifice religions to keep man earthbound. Jesus was sent by the SPA to save us from the permanent termination of our lives, Jesus is Christ, the savior, Satan is the Antichrist, the terminator of life. Every time Satan succeeds in seducing a human to perpetrate his evil schemes , his power grows stronger, so he is constantly on the look out for morally weak humans to carry out his evil seductions.

I know exactly Satan's power because I am living witness to his manifestations. I will never forget those three torturous months of my ordeal against him, and I know that it was through the SPA's intervention that I succeeded in overcoming the power of Satan because I gave up the fight in the end and that was when my ordeal ended because the SPA came to my rescue. I wrote the entire account of my ordeal with Satan in my succeeding books, but Satan is doing everything in his power to block my story from being heard because it is the key to his perdition. The key that was dropped by my feet when I was half awake and half-asleep dreaming that I was Catherine of Aragon late at night on Christmas day 1997, just before our trip to visit the Mayan temples, is the key that will open the door where we can cast Satan to perdition. It has been a quarter century since the original publication of this book, but I am still ignored. I am retyping my entire manuscript because I cannot find the original that I submitted to Vantage press in 1998 and Vantage Press has been out of business for several years now. I told the publisher who offered to republish this book that this manuscript will be ready on New Year, 2025.

As I said, I am not a writer, I am an Architect who knows nothing about the literary field, but I was compelled to write my story. I could only fall asleep at night after I had written something substantial until I finished typing my entire manuscript. I do not have a literary agent; I don't know how to get one until now. While watching TV, I saw an advertisement of Vantage Press encouraging new authors to self-publish their book and that's how I got the first book I authored – The Book of Life - published. If I remember correctly, I spent close to twenty grand of dollars dealing with this publisher. When Vantage Press went out of business, I wrote another book with the title Pure Gift the Second, after I realized that the name I was baptized with when I was an infant: Pura Regalado y Cailao translates into English as Pure Gift one who also brought light. I really wanted to title my second book, Pure Gift: the Second Coming of Jesus but I couldn't find the courage to face ridicules that may come for claiming that I witnessed the promised second coming of Jesus which I truly did, so I kept the title as Pure Gift the Second. Again, I spent thousands of dollars self-publishing this second book three times with three different publishers one after the other. At first it was with Dorrance Publishing but it failed to get any attention, I got another offer to republish it and I agreed, then Book Trail Agency was the third one that published it in 2021. By that time, I found the courage to face whatever there is to face to announce that I truly witnessed the promised second coming of Jesus and I agreed to the encouragement of Booktrail Agency to publish my third book that I titled: The Second Coming of Jesus, where I spent more thousands of dollars self-publishing my book. This last publisher abandoned me, their telephone number was disconnected, the email address I have of them is invalid, their publisher's name is not even mentioned in my book.

My friends were able to order my books from Amazon, so I called Amazon to ask about the whereabouts of my books because I was not getting any sales report. Amazon refused to deal with me because their authorized contact is my publisher. I did not pursue the case with Amazon because I did not want them to stop marketing my book since my primary purpose is to enlighten humanity of the truths revealed to me by the SPA. The truth that all differences in belief systems of all organized religions were caused by manifestations of archetypes created by collective false beliefs that emanated from the collective unconscious of mankind. All organized religions are flawed with false beliefs and the SPA gave me the task of eradicating all false beliefs, false prophets and false gods to unify the belief of all of humanity to end all conflicts and wars.

This was me when I finished writing my book in 1999. At age 55.

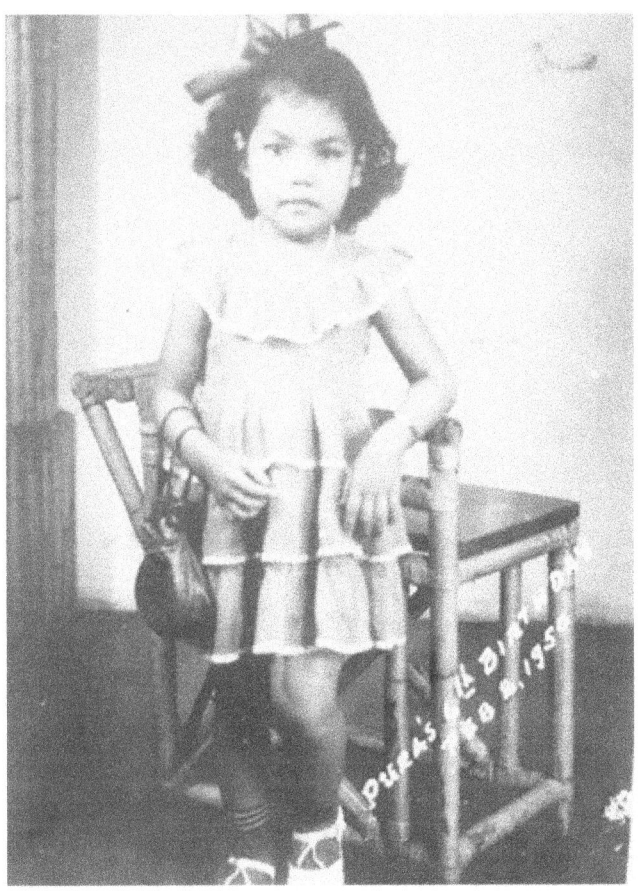

This is my photo when I was six years old, the oldest proof of my real date of birth aside from my Philippine driver's license. The government municipal building where my original birth certificate was issued was bombed and it burned down during the Second World War where all records of births were destroyed. When I applied for my passport for the first time to come to the United States, the date of my birth was mistyped. I did not have the time to demand corrections at that time because I already had my plane ticket, and I did not want to delay my flight. I was not expecting that I would become a permanent resident of USA, My intention was just to help my sister have her baby and then go back home to the Philippines, but the SPA had a different plan for me. I ended up becoming a permanent resident of the USA, I have lived most of my adult life in this country. All my records in the Philippines indicate my true date of birth which is February 2.

1944. Since my Philippine passport had the mistyped date of birth, this became my legal date of birth on all my records in the United States when I became a naturalized United States citizen. On one of my visits to the Philippines, I checked my records in the Philippine Social Security System to find out that when all records were transformed into electronic files, my date of birth was again mistyped that my true records could not be found, that's another Filipino incompetence. I worked at the Philippine Social Security System before I came to the United States, when all records were filed the hard copy way. At that time, I checked my records, and they were accurately filed.

I took a selfie on New Year's Eve of 2025. I will soon be age 81 on February 2, 2025. On my last annual checkup, my PCP told me that everything is the way it should be, keep doing what you're doing. At age 80 I am on zero medication, I'm not taking any pill whatsoever, not even vitamins nor dietary supplements. All my nutrients are from my diet. You be the judge how I am doing with my quest to prove John

3;16 to be literally true.

I decided to merge my two books Pure Gift the Second and The Second coming of Jesus into one with the title Pure Gift: The Second Coming of Jesus which I self-published this year 2024. I am in the waiting period to see if this book will finally be noticed.

After the fly leaf of my original book The Book of life, I urged my readers to make this pledge: I pledge to uphold all the laws of harmony in our universe and dedicate my life to the full pursuit of happiness for all mankind avoiding all activities that will lead to the destruction of our Planet Earth. I also pledge to devote my life to the pursuit of the ultimate perfection of my mind, body and soul until I evolve into the highest level of existence possible to reach the kingdom of immortal omnipotence of the Supreme Power Above. Please include my name in the Book of Life.

Revelation 14:15 Thrust in thy sickle and reap: for the time is come for thee to reap: for the harvest of the earth is ripe.